In police custody: police powers and suspects' rights under the revised PACE codes of practice

by
Tom Bucke and David Brown

A Research and Statistics Directorate Report

Home Office
Research and
Statistics
Directorate

London: Home Office

Home Office Research Studies

The Home Office Research Studies are reports on research undertaken by or on behalf of the Home Office. They cover the range of subjects for which the Home Secretary has responsibility. Titles in the series are listed at the back of this report (copies are available from the address on the back cover). Other publications produced by the Research and Statistics Directorate include Research Findings, the Research Bulletin, Statistical Bulletins and Statistical Papers.

The Research and Statistics Directorate

The Directorate consists of three Units which deal with research and statistics on Crime and Criminal Justice, Offenders and Corrections, Immigration and General Matters; the Programme Development Unit; the Economics Unit; and the Operational Research Unit.

The Research and Statistics Directorate is an integral part of the Home Office, serving the Ministers and the department itself, its services, Parliament and the public through research, development and statistics. Information and knowledge from these sources informs policy development and the management of programmes; their dissemination improves wider public understanding of matters of Home Office concern.

First published 1997

Application for reproduction should be made to the Information and Publications Group, Room 201, Home Office, 50 Queen Anne's Gate, 36 London SW1H 9AT.

Foreword

The Police and Criminal Evidence Act 1984 (PACE) addresses the central stages of the criminal investigation process from crime to trial. The Act and the accompanying Codes of Practice set out police powers and procedures in the investigation of crime and rights of suspects to the point of charge. Revisions to the Codes of Practice were introduced on 10 April 1995 to take account of the recommendations from the Royal Commission on Criminal Justice, the Criminal Justice and Public Order Act 1994 and other related developments. These led to significant changes to police powers in relation to: stop and search; the right of silence; the taking of body samples for forensic analysis; and identification procedures.

This report assesses the extent to which the new provisions are used, examines to whom they are applied, and evaluates any resulting changes with reference to previous research findings. The opportunity was also taken to examine changes relating to suspects in police custody: for example, the new powers available to the police to place conditions on bail after charge and the introduction of 'accredited legal representatives'. Lastly, the report provides information on a number of areas covered by the Codes of Practice which are of interest to those concerned with PACE's effectiveness. These include requests for legal advice and the provision of 'appropriate adults' for vulnerable suspects.

CHRISTOPHER NUTTALL
Director of Research and Statistics

September 1997

Acknowledgements

This study would not have been possible without the co-operation and assistance of a great number of people. We would like to thank the liaison officers appointed in each police force who helped us arrange our research and eased our access into the selected police stations. Our fieldwork was generally free of problems due to the co-operation we received from officers in charge of stations, duty inspectors, custody officers, investigating officers and many others too numerous to name. These people accepted our presence and our demands despite their many commitments and their busy working lives.

We are also very grateful to the team of observers who did a wonderful job on what was a long and very demanding project. They were: Jo Bartlett, Nicki Boldogh, Tamsen Courtenay, Ian Hearden, Zoë James, Tiggey May and Jason Preece. Custody areas are not the most pleasant places to work in, but the observers' professionalism and commitment meant the fieldwork ran far more smoothly than we thought possible. Many hours were also spent deciphering custody records and completing data collection forms. Once again we are grateful to them for carrying out a task which although boring and repetitive, was an essential part of the project.

TOM BUCKE
DAVID BROWN

Contents

Summary

This report looks at recent changes in the treatment of people in police custody. The PACE Codes of Practice, which outline how the police should deal with those in detention, were revised in April 1995, in response to the recommendations of the Royal Commission on Criminal Justice, the Criminal Justice and Public Order Act 1994 and other related developments. The revisions reflected a number of important changes to the treatment of suspects, with the most notable concerning the right of silence and police powers to take body samples for forensic analysis. The study looks at the impact of these revisions and also examines other related changes. These include the placing of conditions on police bail and the introduction of 'accredited legal representatives' by the Law Society in an attempt to improve the legal advice received by suspects. Lastly, the report provides information on a number of important areas regulated by the Codes including requests for legal advice and the provision of 'appropriate adults' for vulnerable suspects.

The research was conducted at 25 police stations in ten forces. The study used three forms of data collection: observation in police custody areas; analysis of custody records; and the administration of questionnaires to investigating officers. The main findings were as follows.

Appropriate adults

- Nearly one in five detainees were juveniles (19%). The vast majority of these had an appropriate adult attend the police station while they were in custody. Well over half of appropriate adults attending police stations were parents or guardians, and just under a quarter were social workers.

- Two per cent of detainees were initially treated as mentally disordered or handicapped. Appropriate adults attended in about two-thirds of these cases. Social workers most frequently acted as appropriate adults.

- It was rare for custody officers to provide guidance to appropriate adults, while those acting in this role rarely asked for an explanation of what was required of them.

- Social workers were more supportive towards the suspect and more co-operative with the police when acting as appropriate adults than family members, who could express high levels of hostility and distress.

Legal advice

- Detainees are increasingly likely to request legal advice while in custody. Four out of ten suspects asked for legal advice, with a notable increase found among juveniles.

- Although 40 per cent of suspects *requested* legal advice only 34 per cent of suspects actually *received* legal advice while in custody. The most common reasons for legal advice not being received were because suspects: changed their minds about needing advice; were released before an advisor arrived; or agreed to see a solicitor later in court rather than at the police station. No cases were found where custody officers had delayed access to legal advice on the basis that it might hinder related investigations.

- Compared to previous studies, the proportion of unqualified 'legal representatives' giving advice to suspects appears to have declined, with a corresponding rise in the number of solicitors giving advice and the introduction of 'accredited representatives'. Accredited representatives were most likely to give advice when a suspect's own legal adviser had been requested.

- Just under half of all suspects interviewed by the police received legal advice while in custody. The rate at which legal advisers attend police interviews has risen compared to previous studies.

The right of silence

- Fifty-eight per cent of those interviewed made confessions to the police. The proportion of suspects making confessions appears to have remained broadly the same since the provisions concerning the inferences from silence were introduced.

- Comparison with past research indicates a significant reduction in the use of the right of silence. Suspects were found both to be less likely to give complete 'no comment' interviews and to refuse questions selectively. The greatest decline in the use of silence was among those receiving legal advice.

- Five per cent of those interviewed were given either a s36 or s37 special warning when they failed to answer questions about certain incriminating circumstances, such as their presence at the scene of a crime. Relatively few responded by giving a satisfactory explanation for the incriminating circumstances.

Body samples for forensic analysis

- *Non-intimate samples* were taken in a very small proportion of cases (7%). However sampling was higher among the targeted offences involving violence against the person (20%), sexual offences (28%) or burglary (19%). The majority of suspects providing non-intimate samples gave their consent.

- *Intimate samples* were taken in less than one per cent of cases, usually in serious offences such as murder, rape and robbery. Blood was by far the most common form of intimate sample taken.

Body searches and identification parades

- Three per cent of suspects were *strip searched*, with over half of these having been arrested in relation to supplying or possessing controlled drugs. Such searches had a low success rate: around one search in eight led to any items being found.

* Less than one per cent of suspects were given an *intimate search.* Such searches were connected with violent acquisitive crimes, such as aggravated burglary and robbery, or drug offences. Little information was available about the outcome of these searches.

* A small number of suspects bailed pending an identification parade were said to have changed their appearance prior to the parade. In these circumstances officers tended to use various strategies to circumvent any changes, such as asking suspects to shave off newly grown beards or moustaches. However, suspects and witnesses failing to appear on the appointed date were said to be a greater factor in the failure of identification procedures.

Disposals

- Just over half of all suspects were charged, 15 per cent were cautioned, 19 per cent had no further action taken, and the remaining 13 per cent transferred or released.

- Comparison with a similar study carried out shortly before the CJPOA reveals that differences in the disposal of juvenile and adult suspects are now much smaller. Juvenile suspects are now:

  - less likely to be bailed for enquiries or reported for summons;
  - less likely to be cautioned (from 34 to 26%)
  - more likely to be charged (from 33 to 40%).

- Comparison with previous research indicates that the level of charging for serious or moderate offences remains broadly the same. However, the figure for minor offences appears to have declined noticeably, with a corresponding rise in cases having no further action taken.

Bail after charge

- Of those suspects charged, 63 per cent were bailed unconditionally, 17 per cent were bailed with conditions, and 20 per cent were detained in custody. The refusal of bail and the granting of bail with conditions occurred at broadly the same rate for juveniles and adults.

- The introduction of police bail with conditions has had only a limited impact on detention after charge. Instead, conditions appear mainly to be placed on those suspects who would in the past have been bailed unconditionally.

- Bail with conditions was most likely to be given in serious offences against the person. There were significant variations in its use between stations.

- The most common conditions attached to police bail were not to contact victims or witnesses, and to keep away from certain, named places. The main reasons given for these conditions were to prevent offending on bail and interference with justice.

1 Introduction

The Police and Criminal Evidence Act 1984 (PACE) has been described as 'the single most significant landmark in the modern development of police powers' (Reiner, 1992). This Act deals with all stages of the investigative process from crime to trial and seeks to strike a balance between the powers of the police and the suspect's rights. Under the Act the Home Secretary is required to issue Codes of Practice which reiterate police powers and explain how they should be exercised. The Codes of Practice cover five areas central to police work, which are: stop and search; search and seizure of property; the detention, treatment and questioning of suspects; identification; and the tape recording of interviews. The Codes detail police powers, suspects' rights and the duties of the police concerning those in detention. Since the introduction of PACE a number of important developments concerning police powers have resulted in the Codes of Practice being revised twice. This report addresses some of the most recent changes to the Codes of Practice and examines their impact.

Revisions to the Codes of Practice were introduced on 10 April 1995 to take account of developments concerning police powers. These included the report of the Royal Commission on Criminal Justice (RCCJ) which made a series of recommendations on police investigations and safeguards for suspects. A number of these along with other important measures were implemented in the Criminal Justice and Public Order Act (CJPOA) 1994. In particular, this Act made significant changes to police powers in relation to: stop and search; the right of silence; the taking of body samples for forensic analysis; and identification procedures. The new and amended sections of the Codes of Practice give instructions on how these powers should be exercised by the police. The study's main aim was to examine the new provisions concerning those in police detention. This included assessing the extent to which the new provisions were used, examining to whom the new provisions were applied, and evaluating any changes with reference to previous research findings. The study had two other aims. The first was to examine changes not included in the revised Codes of Practice. The most important of these concern the police's ability to now attach conditions to bail, and the introduction of 'accredited legal representatives' who can now provide legal advice to suspects in police custody. The second was to provide information on a number of areas regulated by the Codes of Practice which are of interest to those concerned with PACE's effectiveness. These include requests for legal advice and the provision of 'appropriate adults' for vulnerable suspects. The study therefore makes references to previous work on PACE in order to identify trends across these areas. Comparisons are made in particular with a piece of research conducted in the period leading up to the changes examined by this report. This is Phillips and Brown's study (forthcoming) which was based on a sample of people in custody between September 1993 and March 1994. Comparisons are also made with Brown's (1989) earlier study of PACE Codes of Practice which was based upon a sample of detainees held in custody during March 1987.

Methodology

The study used three main forms of data collection: observation of the processing of suspects and detainees[1] in custody areas; analysis of custody records; and administration of questionnaires to investigating officers. In addition, a number of interviews were conducted with officers responsible for identification procedures. The research was conducted at 25 police stations in the ten forces listed below:

Bedfordshire	Leicestershire	Nottinghamshire
Cambridgeshire	Metropolitan Police	West Midlands
Greater Manchester	Northamptonshire	Hampshire
Northumbria.		

The forces included county and metropolitan forces, while the stations could be categorised as city centre, inner-city and large town. Details of the three forms of data collection are outlined below.

The observed sample

This component of the study provided first-hand information on police practice in dealing with detainees. Observation was conducted in the custody areas of 13 police stations[2] with Home Office observers present in the custody area every day between the hours of 0900 and midnight (later if it was busy) for a period of three weeks. A minimum of 315 hours observation was therefore carried out at each station leading to a total of, at least, 4,095 hours for all 13 stations. During this time 3,950 detainees passed through police custody. The fieldwork period ran from the middle of August 1995 until the end of February 1996. Both quantitative and qualitative data

---

1   In this report the term 'suspects' refers to people arrested under suspicion of committing a criminal offence and whose detention is regulated by the Codes of Practice. The term 'detainees' refers to both suspects and those in detention who are not under suspicion, including those arrested on a warrant for failing to appear at court or to pay a fine, and those in custody under the Mental Health Act 1983.

2   These were: Luton (Bedfordshire); Peterborough (Cambridgeshire); Beaumont Leys (Leicestershire); Rochdale and Stretford (Greater Manchester); Southampton (Hampshire); Croydon and Hackney (Metropolitan Police); Campbell Square (Northamptonshire); Gateshead (Northumbria); Radford Road (Nottinghamshire); Queens Road and Wolverhampton (West Midlands).

were collected on appropriate adults, searches, legal advice, the taking of body samples, police interviews, bail and case outcomes. Reasons for arrest and demographic details of the detainee were also recorded.

Conducting observational work on the police raises questions about the effect it may have on the behaviour of those being studied (see Phillips and Brown, 1997). Police officers may change their everyday routines, so that the observer gets a false impression of what is thought to be 'real' practice. However, there are a number of reasons why an 'observer effect' was unlikely to be significant. Firstly, for custody officers (the main focus of observation) to change their routine over the prolonged period of observation would be troublesome and unduly time-consuming. Furthermore, it would be difficult not to slip back into previous ways of performing tasks, especially during busy periods. Secondly, the research was not generally viewed as a threat by officers. While remaining objective, observers usually enjoyed good relations with custody personnel: for example, allowing officers to see copies of the data collection forms. As the observation proceeded it became clear the focus of the research was not on the performance of individual officers but on the general implementation of the new provisions. Thirdly, the main findings could be checked against the custody record sample in order to identify any anomalies.

The investigating officer sample

A self-completion questionnaire was given to the police officer responsible for each case in the observation sample. The observers were responsible for issuing the questionnaire and for ensuring that it was returned. The questionnaire's central focus was upon police interviews. It included questions on admissions made by suspects, the right to silence, and 'special warnings' which can now be given to suspects under certain circumstances. The questionnaires were returned in 90 per cent of cases (3,537 out of 3,950).

The custody record sample

The Codes of Practice state that a custody record must be opened for each person brought to a police station under arrest, or arrested at a station having attended voluntarily (C 2.1).[3] These records provide details on those detained and chart all the main events concerning the detainee's time in custody. In this study, custody records were analysed because they offered an effective way of collecting data on a large number of police detainees. Furthermore, enough records were analysed to allow an examination of

---

3   In this report when a specific reference is made to the Codes of Practice the particular section is cited in brackets.

fairly rare procedures, such as body searches and the taking of body samples.

A total of 12,500 custody records were analysed, making it one of the largest samples of police detainees ever undertaken in this country. The sample was draw from 25 police stations with 500 custody records analysed at each station. Custody records were sampled at the 13 stations where observation was carried out and at another 12 stations.[4]

Custody records were sampled from the beginning of June 1995, two months after the revised Codes come into effect thereby allowing officers time to become familiar with the changes. This meant that the time periods covered by the observation and custody record samples did not overlap. In addition to demographic material and reasons for arrest, data was collected on legal advice, police interviews, medical attention, photographs, appropriate adults, searches, body samples, bail and case outcome.

Structure of the report

This report is divided into eight chapters. Chapter 2 examines the treatment of vulnerable groups and focuses on the role of appropriate adults and the provision of medical attention. Chapter 3 addresses requests for legal advice, how advice was given, the type of legal adviser consulted and the extent of consultations. Chapter 4 focuses upon police interviews, confessions and the right of silence. Identification and investigation procedures, including body samples, body searches, the use of photographs and identification procedures are dealt with in Chapter 5. Chapter 6 details the outcome of detention and Chapter 7 investigates the decisions the police make concerning bail for those charged. Details of the changes to the Codes of Practice and related developments are outlined in each relevant chapter. The conclusions of the report are presented in Chapter 8.

---

4   The additional 12 stations were: Bedford (Bedfordshire); Cambridge (Cambridgeshire); Basingstoke (Hampshire); Charles Street (Leicestershire); Lewisham and Romford (Metropolitan Police); Corby (Northamptonshire); Newcastle West and Newcastle East (Northumbria); Nottingham Central (Nottinghamshire); Brierley Hill and Coventry (West Midlands).

2 Vulnerable groups in detention

This chapter examines detainees who required assistance while in custody due to their age or health (physical or mental). The first part of the chapter focuses upon the use of 'appropriate adults' to safeguard the interests of juveniles and mentally disordered[1] or mentally handicapped people while in detention. The second part of the chapter deals with medical treatment given to those in custody. The Codes of Practice state that if a detainee appears to be suffering from physical illness or injury or mental health problems the custody officer should immediately call for the police surgeon (C 9.2). Here the extent to which detainees received medical attention is examined, along with the reasons for such attention and the recommendations resulting from it.

Appropriate adults

Under PACE the police must provide an 'appropriate adult' for juvenile and mentally disordered or mentally handicapped detainees (C 3.9). The role of the appropriate adult is to provide support to a vulnerable person in custody which may involve:

- giving advice

- ensuring police interviews are conducted properly

- facilitating communication between officers and the detainee.

A person, including a parent or guardian, should not be an appropriate adult if he or she is involved in the offence, for example as a suspect, witness or victim (C 1C). People acting as solicitors or lay visitors should also not be appropriate adults (C 1F). Furthermore, admissions made by a suspect to an appropriate adult do not have the same status as those made to a legal adviser, and therefore can be disclosed to the police. In cases where the detainee appears to be suffering from a mental disorder, PACE states that in

---

1   The term 'mental disorder' is used throughout the Codes of Practice and is defined by the Mental Health Act 1983 as 'mental illness, arrested or incomplete development of mind, psychopathic disorder and any other disorder or disability of mind' (C 1G).

addition to an appropriate adult being contacted the police must call in a registered medical practitioner and an approved social worker to assess the detainee at the police station (C 3.10).

Juveniles

Nearly one in five detainees (19%) in the custody record sample were under 17 years of age. However, this proportion varied widely between stations, with juveniles making up only 12 per cent of suspects at Hackney compared to 34 per cent at Radford Road. Ninety-one per cent of juveniles had an appropriate adult in attendance for all or some of their time in custody.

Figure 2.1 shows who acted as an appropriate adult for juvenile suspects. In the majority of cases this was a parent or guardian (59%), with other relatives attending in a much smaller number of cases (8%). A social worker attended in just under a quarter of cases (23%). While past work has raised the possibility of social workers being increasingly asked to act as appropriate adults (Brown et al., 1992; Evans and Rawstorne, 1994), figures from a series of studies suggest no discernable trend during the 1990s. The use of social workers as appropriate adults tends to fluctuate at around a quarter of all juvenile cases, with the present study's figure falling between those previously given by Brown et al. (1992) (28%) and Phillips and Brown (forthcoming) (20%).

Figure 2.1 Identity of appropriate adults for juvenile detainees

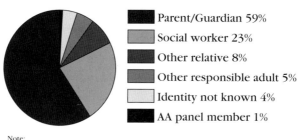

Parent/Guardian 59%
Social worker 23%
Other relative 8%
Other responsible adult 5%
Identity not known 4%
AA panel member 1%

Note:
1. Sample size = 2,190 (juvenile detainees with appropriate adult attending).

In one per cent of cases, those attending the station were members of an appropriate adult panel. These panels are found in certain parts of the country and are made up of lay people who are on call to represent the interests of vulnerable suspects. Five per cent of cases involved another responsible adult such as a family friend or neighbour, while in four per cent of cases the appropriate adult's identity was not known.

Most appropriate adults attended a station having been contacted by the police (77%). Fourteen per cent arrived with the person entering custody, probably because the police arrested the juvenile at their home address, or collected their parents before taking the juvenile to the police station. For nine per cent of juveniles an appropriate adult was not found, with the reason in a third of cases being that a parent or guardian refused to attend the police station. It was unclear in the remaining two-thirds of cases why an appropriate adult did not attend. While these juveniles had mostly been arrested for notifiable offences, they appeared to be treated differently to other suspects, with few being interviewed or charged during their time in custody.[2]

Mentally disordered or mentally handicapped people

Compared to juveniles, mentally disordered or mentally handicapped detainees made up a much smaller group of those in detention. Just two per cent of all those in the custody record sample were treated as being mentally disordered or mentally handicapped. Other research has suggested that the proportion who are actually mentally disordered might be higher and that detainees with mental health problems are not always identified by custody officers. These studies, using independent medical assessments and various definitions of mental problems, have estimated that those suffering from mental disorder or mental handicap make up between 10 per cent and 26 per cent of detainees (see Gudjunsson et al.; 1993 and Robertson et al.; 1995).

Compared to other detainees, those classified as having mental problems tended to be older and were more likely to be women. Forty-three per cent were over 30 years of age, compared to 27 per cent of other detainees, while 24 per cent were women compared to 15 per cent of the whole sample. There was little variation across stations in the proportions of detainees treated as having mental problems. Four out of ten of these detainees were in custody under s.136 of the Mental Health Act 1983 (MHA), with the police station providing 'a place of safety'. The remainder had been arrested for a wide range of crimes, with theft, criminal damage and public order offences the most common.

---

2   Annex C of Code C states that the interviewing of vulnerable suspects without an appropriate adult present can only take place under certain urgent circumstances and with the consent of an officer of superintendent rank or above.

Appropriate adults attended the police station in two-thirds of cases (66%) involving mentally disordered detainees, a much lower proportion than that for juveniles. Custody records provided a number of explanations for why in the remaining one-third of cases an adult was not called. In a very small number of cases a parent or social worker refused to attend the station. In the majority of cases a doctor attended the station and recommended that an appropriate adult was not required or that the detainee was fit to be kept in custody and interviewed. It should be noted however, that the requirement for an appropriate adult is independent from that for a doctor and the police should not wait for a doctor's recommendation where they suspect a detainee has mental problems. In other cases custody officers appeared to have viewed the detainee's condition as not serious enough to require an appropriate adult, or their initial concerns receded.

Confirming previous studies, social workers were far more likely to act as appropriate adults in cases involving mentally disordered or mentally handicapped detainees than in those involving juveniles. Figure 2.2 shows the identity of those attending the police station. Six out of ten cases involved a social worker, these being equally divided between duty social workers, specialist social workers and social workers whose status was unknown. Friends or neighbours and parents or guardians acted as appropriate adults in most of the remaining cases.

Figure 2.2 Identity of appropriate adults for mentally disordered/ mentally handicapped detainees

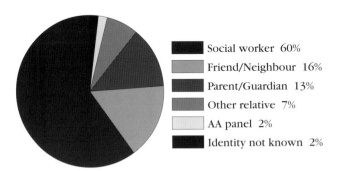

- Social worker 60%
- Friend/Neighbour 16%
- Parent/Guardian 13%
- Other relative 7%
- AA panel 2%
- Identity not known 2%

Note:
1. Sample size = 165 (mentally disordered handicapped detainees who had appropriate adult attend).

In addition to securing an appropriate adult, PACE requires the attendance of a doctor in cases where a detainee appears to be suffering from mental problems or has been detained under the MHA (C 3.10). In the custody record sample a doctor attended in just over three-quarters of such cases (76%), a higher proportion than that found by Brown et al. (1992). While such medical attention focused on the nature and extent of any mental problem, in a small number of cases it also concerned other medical matters, including physical injuries, drunkenness, drug addiction and medical conditions. The recommendations resulting from a doctor attending the station are outlined in Figure 2.3. In over a third of cases an appropriate adult was recommended, while in just under a third one was thought not to be required. An equally common recommendation was that the detainee was fit to be kept in custody, while less frequent recommendations were that the detained person was fit for interview, required hospital attention, should be allowed medication, or should be given regular checks while held in custody.

Figure 2.3 Outcome of medical attention for mentally disordered/ mentally handicapped detainees

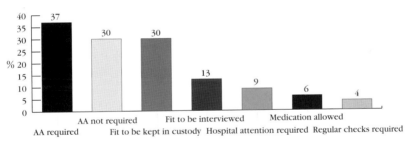

Notes:
1. Percentages do not add up to 100 per cent due to multiple reasons given.
2. Sample size = 190 (cases where doctor provided medical attention).

The role and function of appropriate adults

The Codes of Practice do not require appropriate adults to be informed about their role having arrived at the police station. Custody officers are required to outline the role of an appropriate adult *to the detainee*, stating that this person is there to assist and advise them while in custody and that they therefore may meet in private if they wish (C 3.12). When an interview is to be conducted the appropriate adult be told that his or her role is to advise the suspect, to observe that the interview is conducted properly, and to facilitate communication with the person being questioned (C 11.16).

Various commentators have highlighted the difficulties faced by both social workers and family members when acting as appropriate adults (Palmer, 1996; Brown et al., 1992; Dixon et al., 1990; Thomas, 1988). Adults attending a police station may be unclear about their role, and when told, may find it hard to put into practice. They may encounter contradictions in their role, most notably in regard to the right of silence, when the need to advise may run counter to the need to facilitate communication (Dixon et al., 1990). Furthermore, like detainees, parents and even some social workers, may be disorientated, anxious and acquiescent to police requests once in the police station. In light of these possible difficulties, the observed sample examined both the advice appropriate adults received from the police and their actions in the custody area.

The level of instruction given to appropriate adults in cases involving juveniles or mentally disordered/mentally handicapped people was limited. In cases where those in custody were treated as suspects and were interviewed by officers, a division was found between family members (parents, guardians and relatives) and social workers. Twenty-nine per cent of family members received some form of explanation of their role from custody officers, compared to four per cent of social workers. As the observation was limited to the custody area, the study cannot say how much instruction was given to appropriate adults during police interviews.

These figures suggest that officers assume social workers understand the role of appropriate adult and do not require an explanation. Previous research suggests that this is not always the case (Evans and Rawstorne, 1994; Palmer and Hart, 1996). The low level of briefing for family members may sometimes be due to those attending having attended on a previous occasion. Certainly, some parents and relatives were so used to attending the police station that they were on familiar terms with officers. However, officers should not assume that appropriate adults are conversant with their role, even if they have acted in such a position before. In addition the Codes of Practice do not stipulate who should brief the appropriate adult. As stated above this may have been done by the investigating officer at the start of an interview and therefore away from researchers. However, other research indicates that this very rarely happens (Evans, 1993), and by this stage it would be too late for the appropriate adult to have a private discussion with the suspect.

Overall, these possibilities are unlikely to account for all those cases where appropriate adults attending were given no explanation of their role. In addition, those attending were unlikely to ask officers for an explanation, with only five per cent of family members and two per cent of social workers doing so. Where the position of the appropriate adult is not clearly spelled out the danger is that the role recedes to one involving a passive adult presence where little or no assistance is offered to the detainee.

A related issue is the suitability of those acting as appropriate adults. Dixon et al. (1990) describe how some parents disregard their role and deliberately help the police to obtain confessions from their children, while Palmer and Hart (1996) suggest that parents unclear about their role can unwittingly become agents of the interviewing officers. In order to examine the competence of appropriate adults, the observers were asked to characterise the disposition of the appropriate adult in relation to both the detainee and the police. Table 2.1 outlines the demeanour of family members and social workers acting as appropriate adults for juvenile suspects.

Table 2.1 Appropriate adult's demeanour towards juvenile suspects and police

Demeanour	Family members %	Social workers %
Towards the suspect		
Co-operative/supportive	26	45
Calm	12	14
Neutral	30	39
Distressed	24	2
Hostile/unsupportive	8	0
Towards the police		
Co-operative/supportive	49	60
Calm	10	15
Neutral	31	23
Distressed	5	1
Hostile/unsupportive	5	1

Note:
1. Sample size= 415 (family members), 211 (social workers).

One clear finding from Table 2.1 is that family members tend to be less co-operative or supportive towards juvenile suspects compared to social workers. Instead family members often expressed hostility and distress towards the suspect (emotions which were rarely reported for social workers). In regard to the demeanour of appropriate adults towards the police, Table 2.1 shows social workers to be more co-operative and calm compared to family members. Some family members were described as expressing hostility or distress towards the police but these were at lower levels than those expressed towards suspects. Very few social workers were reported to have such dispositions.

The issue of hostility from family members is illustrated by the observers' field notes. Clearly parents and relatives have a right to be distressed under such circumstances, but the issue is whether the reaction to a juvenile's arrest in some cases undermines a family member's ability to act as an appropriate adult. In many cases family members were obviously very upset with the juvenile in detention, but were still capable of fulfilling their role. For example:

> *Case no. 03-05-00144: Mother very annoyed having waited two hours in police station. Angry with son: 'There'll be no Christmas for you!' Overall, unhappy, but aware of responsibility.*

In other cases this was a little less clear:

> *Case no. 07-15-00030: Father cooperative and fairly friendly with police. Very aggressive and quite threatening towards son; had been trying to keep his son away from the estate. Generally angry and increasingly aggressive towards everybody.*

> *Case no. 05-10-00185: Father very angry about whole affair. Raised voices with son after having gone straight into private consultation room. Boy obviously given a good telling off - he had been visibly frightened and crying earlier.*

> *Case no. 10-21-00196: Step-father generally easy going with police officers. However, said to his step-son: "I'm going to bust your ass." Aggressive and threatening, very loud shouting coming from consultation room. Anger eventually subsided and he said he would stay around until it was all over.*

The anger of some family members was so strong they appeared to be unable to fulfil the appropriate adult role, and even used physical violence against the juvenile:

Case no. 08-18-00184: On arrival in the custody area the mother gave a series of excuses for her son's behaviour. When son emerged from his cell she hit him several times round the head. Very angry. Custody officer took her to one side and explained that this was not the behaviour of an appropriate adult. Mother told to leave and father asked to attend station instead.

Case no. 10-21-00222: Parent crying and very upset with juvenile. Tried to attack detainee and restrained by officers.

In addition to being unable to advise and assist, such family members are likely to add further pressure to that already being faced by suspects during detention and police questioning.

Some family members arrived at the police station clearly drunk, and while no violence was reported in these cases, it was unclear to what extent the appropriate adult understood what was happening or was able to assist the juvenile. Another reaction from family members was indifference, with a lack of support for and co-operation with the juvenile detainee meaning that the appropriate adult role was barely fulfilled:

Case no. 07-15-00499: Mother not outwardly upset but totally ignored her son. Did not say a word to detainee and left to wait in police station's front office after very short period of time in custody area.

Case no. 08-17-00269: Mother spent time in custody area reading book and eating snacks. Totally indifferent to police, suspect and whole situation.

Case no. 10-21-00129: Step-father argumentative and hostile towards police. Did not communicate with step-son. Racist comments towards officer and generally antagonistic towards everyone.

A similar situation could occur when the parent or relative of a juvenile arrested with the suspect was asked to act as an appropriate adult. Such an arrangement could be convenient to officers when a juvenile's own parents could not be contacted or refused to assist, and when a social worker could take some time to arrive. However, as the following cases show, such people are not guaranteed to have the commitment that a family member or social worker might have:

Case no. 07-15-00185: Mother of suspect refused to attend station. Mother of co-arrestee fairly annoyed but obliged police by acting as appropriate adult. However, did not sit in on legal consultation. Only did the minimum.

Case no. 05-10-00090: Mother of co-arrestee performing appropriate adult role, said nothing to juvenile except 'hello'.

When parents have acted as appropriate adults there have clearly been different interpretations of their role in terms of providing advice to the suspect and aiding communication:

Case no. 10-21-00158: Mother with suspects on their arrival at station. Argumentative with officers and tells daughters to deny everything.

Case no. 01-04-00067: Mother very co-operative with the police but very unhappy with son. Called son a 'liar' when answering police questions.

Case no. 06-12-00185: Parents co-operative with officers - asked the custody officer to give their 'lad the fright of his life'. Both very concerned about suspect. Told son to tell the truth.

In other cases appropriate adults were confused either by their role or by the procedures they needed to understand in order to fulfil it:

Case no. 04-09-00006: Father puzzled by role of appropriate adult. Officers try to explain that if father speaks to his son in private and his son admits something to him, then he cannot act as AA. Heated discussion then followed.

Case no. 07-15-00121: Suspect returning to police custody after being bailed for enquiries. Father inquisitive - didn't understand exactly what had happened between his son being bailed and being charged. Custody officer explained evidence etc. Father co-operative and friendly with officers. Obviously had not been an appropriate adult before. Had problems understanding legal side of proceedings and his role.

The Codes of Practice (C 1.7) state that an appropriate adult must be aged 18 years or over to ensure that those taking on this role are mature enough to fulfil it. However, in a number of cases, while the person acting as an appropriate adult may have been aged 18 years or over, their maturity for this role was open to question:

Case no. 05-10-00097: Friend arrived with detainee and acted as appropriate adult. Seemed a bit of a 'scallywag' himself. Chatted to another detainee whom he knew. Just stood there biting his nails, going through the motions. Unconcerned. Told off by custody sergeant for being foolish and joking around. Hardly 'appropriate'!

Case no. 05-10-00160: Suspect's baby-sitter sent by mother following police contact. Seemed very young herself. Didn't seem too sure of what was going on. But obviously knew suspect. Had a private consultation.

In at least one case the use of a young appropriate adult raised questions beyond those concerning maturity:

Case no. 10-21-00067: Detainee's sister attended station after police contact. Relaxed and calm with police. Note: after initial contact with solicitor emerges that sister is inappropriate. Has knowledge of and possible witness to alleged motor vehicle offences. No other appropriate adult called.

In contrast with family members, social workers appeared to find it easier to fulfil the role of appropriate adult, tending to be more neutral or detached, and less hostile or distressed. The following examples again underline this point:

Case no. 07-28-00422: Co-operative and polite with police officers. Calm and caring with detainee. In general, at ease and understanding to both police and detainee.

Case no. 06-12-00228: Pleasant and co-operative with police. Concerned at suspect's detention, tried to find secure accommodation for juvenile but couldn't. Caring and at ease.

Case no. 08-17-00155: Very quiet but co-operative with officers. Offered to bring the boy back to answer his bail. Not angry or reproachful towards the boy - very at ease.

Social workers tended to provide a calm and more dispassionate approach compared to family members, and by being more detached were unlikely to be involved in some of the problems raised above. However, other research has indicated problems concerning social workers including a lack of training and a confusion about the appropriate adult role (see Evans and Rawstorne, 1994; Palmer and Hart, 1996).

Medical attention

The Codes of Practice require a police surgeon to be called in all cases where a detainee appears to be physically ill or mentally disordered, is injured, fails to respond normally to questions or conversations, or otherwise appears to need medical attention (C 9.2). Fourteen per cent of detainees in the custody records received medical attention.[3] However wide variations were found between stations, with a quarter of detainees at Bedford police station receiving attention compared to seven per cent of those at Radford Road. These variations partly relate to the location of stations, with those, like Bedford, located in town centres likely to have a large number of cases involving drunkenness and violent disorder connected with the town's nightlife. Variations are also due to custody officers in different stations having their own informal policies on when medical attention should be administered. This is particularly relevant to those detainees who are drunk. In such cases the Codes of Practice recommend that custody officers should err on the side of caution and call for the police surgeon. An assessment can then be made on the extent of intoxication, whether any drugs have been taken, and whether any mental disorder or undetected injuries are present (C 9.B). At Bedford police station custody officers tended to follow this advice, while at other stations specialist medical attention appeared to have been used more selectively.

Overall, a large number of those receiving medical attention had been arrested for acts of violence, public order offences and drunkenness. Figure 2.4 lists the reasons given for medical attention and shows that the most common ones concerned physical injuries and drunkenness, largely sustained in connection with the above offences.

Figure 2.4 Reasons given for medical attention

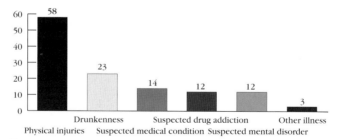

Notes:
1. Percentages do not add up to 100 per cent due to multiple reasons given.
2. Sample size = 1,984 (detainees receiving medical attention).

---

3   Some detainees may enter police custody having already received medical attention, with arresting officers taking those with serious injuries to a local hospital for treatment before proceeding to the police station.

A police surgeon was also required for detainees with medical conditions, such as epilepsy or diabetes and who required prescribed drugs. Such medication may or may not be in a detainee's possession and a doctor would be required to either prescribe medication or advise the custody officers on the use of medicines found on the person in custody. In cases where detainees were believed to be drug addicts, again a doctor would be called and, depending on whether the detainee was a registered addict or not, medication might be prescribed. Medical care was also provided in order to establish whether the detainee was mentally disordered or mentally handicapped, and to treat detainees feeling ill (head and stomach aches being the usual complaints).

In most cases a doctor attended the station (92 per cent) or gave advice over the telephone (four per cent), while officers gave medical treatment on a small number of occasions (four per cent).

Figure 2.5 Outcome of medical attention

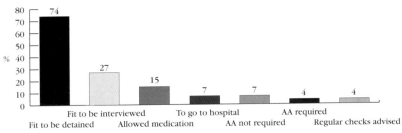

Notes:
1. Percentages do not add up to 100 per cent due to multiple recommendations given.
2. Sample size = 1984 (detainees receiving medical attention).

Figure 2.5 lists the outcome of medical attention in those cases where a doctor attended. Medical attention usually confirmed that detention should continue, with the most common recommendations being that the detainee was fit to be kept in custody and was fit to be interviewed. A break in detention occurred in only a small number of cases where hospital treatment was required. In other cases a recommendation was given on the need for an appropriate adult, medication allowed, and regular checks advised.

Key points

- Nearly one in five detainees were juveniles (19%), with the vast majority of these having an appropriate adult attend the police station while they were in custody. Well over half of appropriate adults attending police stations were parents or guardians of the juvenile detainee, and just under a quarter were social workers.

- Just two per cent of detainees were treated as mentally disordered or mentally handicapped, with appropriate adults attending in about two-thirds of cases. Social workers most frequently acted as appropriate adults, with friends and parents the next most common.

- Doctors assessed around three-quarters of mentally disordered or mentally handicapped detainees, with the most common recommendations concerning whether an appropriate adult was required and whether the detainee was fit to be kept in custody.

- The level of guidance given to appropriate adults by custody officers was limited. Family members and social workers rarely asked for an explanation of their role.

- Social workers were more supportive and co-operative when acting as appropriate adults compared to family members, who could express high levels of hostility and distress. Family members expressed greater levels of hostility towards the police than social workers. An inability to understand the role and the associated procedures were problems for some appropriate adults.

- Fourteen per cent of all detainees were given medical attention during their time in police custody. The majority of these detainees had physical injuries sustained in connection with the offence for which they were arrested.

- When medical attention was required a police surgeon usually attended the station rather than officers giving medical attention. Police surgeons were most likely to make recommendations concerning whether the detainee was fit to remain in custody, or to be interviewed, or whether a prescribed medication should be allowed.

3 Legal advice

The Codes of Practice state that, subject to exceptional circumstances, people in police detention must be told that they can at any time communicate with a legal adviser free of charge (C 6.1). This chapter examines suspects' requests for legal advice and their outcome. Previous studies have shown that the proportion of suspects making requests for legal advice has gradually risen since the introduction of PACE and the current research data is examined in the light of this trend. Under the most recent revisions to the Codes of Practice custody officers are required to ask those refusing legal advice their reasons for doing so (C 6.5) and these responses are outlined. Not all requests for legal advice actually lead to advice being given, and the reasons for its non-provision are described. The chapter also explores how advice was given, the type of legal adviser consulted, and the extent of consultations. One issue examined here is the recent attempt to improve the advice given to suspects by 'legal representatives' through an accreditation scheme.

Requesting legal advice

A number of studies have shown that both the introduction of PACE in 1986 and the first revision of the Codes of Practice in 1991 were marked by rises in requests for legal advice. Pre-PACE studies gave estimates of detainees requesting legal advice which ranged from three to 20 per cent (see Softley et al., 1980; Bottomley et al., 1989; Brown, 1991). The introduction of PACE saw this rise to around 25 per cent (see Brown, 1989; Sanders et al., 1989; Morgan et al., 1991), while the first revised Codes of Practice witnessed a further rise to 32 per cent (see Brown et al., 1992). In line with this trend the custody record sample indicated another rise, with 40 per cent of detainees (those arrested for offences or detained for other reasons) now requesting legal advice.[1]

---

1   The observed sample confirms this figure. Sanders et al. have suggested that custody records tend to under-record requests for legal advice. However these figures suggest, at least in the case of legal advice, that there is little discrepancy between record-keeping and practice.

Previous explanations for the rise in requests for legal advice have highlighted how the Codes of Practice seek to ensure that suspects entering custody understand that legal assistance is available to them free of charge (see Brown et al., 1992). The rise in the request rate may also be due to an increase in requests among juvenile suspects. This group has traditionally been less likely than adults to request legal advice, with Phillips and Brown (forthcoming) finding that 33 per cent of juveniles requested advice against 39 per cent of adults. However, in both the custody record and observation studies juvenile suspects now had a slightly *higher* request rate than adults (both studies: juveniles, 41% adults, 39%). Since juveniles make up a fifth of all suspects, a rise in their request rate will have a noticeable effect on the overall figure.

One explanation for why more juveniles are requesting advice is that many social workers now have a policy of asking for legal advice as a matter of course. In addition, custody officers may be increasingly sensitive to the position of vulnerable suspects in detention and are now sometimes encouraging juveniles to request legal advice. At the same time juvenile suspects may be more aware of their rights due to the rewording of the police caution and changes in the provisions concerning the right of silence.

The majority of suspects making a request did so on arrival (79%), with others either asking for legal advice later on (18%) or arriving at the police station with a solicitor (3%).[2] The request rate for suspects varied widely between stations, with over half of those at Radford Road police station seeking advice, compared to just under a fifth at Wolverhampton. The rate for other detainees varied even more widely, from 70 per cent at Nottingham Central to 18 per cent at Romford. Overall, suspects were marginally less likely to ask for legal advice than other groups of detainees (40% compared to 42%, respectively).

While past distinctions between adult and juvenile suspects appeared to have been erased, differences in request rates were still present across other socio-demographic lines. As revealed in previous research (see Phillips and Brown, forthcoming), female suspects were less likely to request legal advice than male suspects (34% compared to 40%). In terms of ethnicity, Afro-Caribbean and Asian suspects were much more likely to request legal advice (46 and 44% respectively), than white suspects (36%). Such differences are partly grounded in the kinds of offences connected with each group. Women suspects were less likely than men to have been arrested for offences with above average request rates such as burglary and robbery. A high proportion of women suspects had been arrested for prostitution, few of whom sought legal advice. Afro-Caribbeans were more likely to have been arrested for violence against the person, robbery, and fraud and forgery

---

2   Appendix Table A.1 shows the proportion of suspects and other detainees who requested legal advice at each station.

compared to whites, with these offences all having high request rates irrespective of ethnic group. Compared to Afro-Caribbeans and Asians, whites were more likely to have been arrested for public order offences which had a low request rate.

Overall, past studies have shown variations in requests for legal advice to be due to a number of factors. These include:

- the kinds of offences found at each station,[3] with type of offence and level of seriousness important factors in determining requests for legal advice (see Brown, 1989; Phillips and Brown, forthcoming)

- factors centring on the suspect including his or her ethnicity, employment status, physical and mental condition on arrival at the police station, and issues concerning bail and previous convictions (see Phillips and Brown, forthcoming)

- differences in the availability of legal advice between areas (see Brown, 1989)

- the way in which the right to legal advice is conveyed by custody officers to the suspect (see Morgan et al., 1991; Sanders et al., 1989; Bottomley et al., 1989)

- more intangible factors including cultural differences between areas, suspects' views on the usefulness of legal advice emanating from experience and folklore, general views of the police, and the station where the suspect was taken on arrest (see Morgan et al., 1991; Phillips and Brown, forthcoming).

Refusing legal advice

Sixty per cent of suspects decided not to request legal advice. Under the new Codes (C 6.5), custody officers are required to ask about reasons for this decision and to record any response. However, the observation research found that a large number of custody officers simply did not do this. Overall, less than half of those refusing legal advice were asked their reasons. This went beyond cases of minor seriousness, with an extremely wide range of offences involved. At two stations in particular almost none of those refusing advice were asked why, highlighting just how little this practice has been adopted in some areas.

---

3   Appendix Table A.2 presents the proportion of suspects requesting legal advice by offence.

When officers did ask for reasons they did not always get an answer. Overall, a third of suspects in the observed sample did not respond. Table 3.1 presents those reasons given by suspects when they did respond.

Table 3.1 Reasons given for not requesting legal advice

Reason given	%
Not worth it/ Not required/ Not necessary	56
Maybe later/ I'll see how it goes/ I'll wait until my parents arrive/ I'll wait until the breath test	17
Because I'm innocent/ I haven't done anything wrong	11
It would take too long/ Because I want to go home soon/ Don't want to be here all night	4
Because I'm guilty	4
Solicitor already aware/ My parents have gone to get one	1
Other	7
Total	100

Note:
1. Sample size=511 (suspects giving reasons for refusing legal advice).

The most common reason given was that suspects did not feel the situation merited a legal adviser. It is unclear quite why suspects decided that this was the case. One reason might be that the case involved a minor offence for which legal advice was not thought necessary: for example, criminal damage or motoring offences. However, the majority of these suspects had been arrested for offences of moderate seriousness such as theft and shoplifting, while some had been arrested for serious offences involving violence. No differences were found between the proportion of juveniles and adults giving this reason.

The next most common reason for not requesting legal advice was that the suspect would wait until later to make such a decision. Custody officers sometimes encourage this course of action by emphasising to suspects that they can always call a solicitor if they change their mind. These suspects fell into two main groups. The first had been arrested for drink/ driving offences and were waiting for the result of tests for alcohol. The second were juveniles arrested for various forms of theft who were waiting for an appropriate adult to attend the station.

Contact rate for legal advice

The custody record sample found that the vast majority of requests for legal advice led to an adviser being contacted (89%). However, in a small number of cases contact was not made (11).[4] Previous research has estimated the non-contact rate to be higher, with around a quarter of requests not leading to contact with an adviser (Sanders et al., 1989). However, the current study's figure is very close to that given by Phillips and Brown (forthcoming), suggesting that contact rates may have improved during the 1990s, perhaps due to the increased efforts of custody officers or the rise in the use of solicitors' representatives to provide advice at police stations (see McConville et al., 1994).

The non-contact rate varied from two per cent at Peterborough to 21 per cent at Croydon. The most common reasons for non-contact involved the suspect:

- changing his or her mind about needing legal advice

- being released before an advisor arrived

- agreeing to see a solicitor in court rather than at the station.

Reasons given for non-contact were not linked to particular groups of offences.

Under PACE access to legal advice can be formally delayed in serious cases where a senior officer has reasonable grounds to believe that the provision of legal advice will either: lead to people being injured or evidence being interferred with; involve people suspected of committing a crime being alerted; hinder the recovery of property obtained through an offence (see Code C, Annex B). This appears to be an extremely rare occurrence with no such delay found in the custody record sample consisting of 12,500 cases. Previous research found legal advice to be delayed in around one per cent of arrests (see Brown, 1989). However it appears that this power has fallen into disuse after a number of Court of Appeal decisions during the late 1980s clarified the circumstances under which delay is permissible.[5]

---

4   This figure excludes those suspects who arrived at a police station with a legal adviser.
5   **R v. Samuels** (1988) 2 W.L.R.,920–934; **R v. Alladice** (1988) 87 Cr. App. R. 380.

Receiving legal advice

Thirty four per cent of suspects and 27 per cent of other detainees received legal advice while in custody. The strong attrition rate for other detainees is mainly due to those arrested on warrant initially requesting legal advice at the station but then agreeing for a consultation to take place at court the next day. These figures are broadly in line with Phillips and Brown's (forthcoming) study which found that 33 per cent of suspects and 25 per cent of other detainees received legal advice. Figure 3.1 shows that over half of suspects received face-to-face advice at the police station, while just over a quarter received advice at the police station together with a telephone consultation. Just under a fifth of suspects had telephone advice only, but this was a much more common form of consultation for other detainees. This may be because these detainees had been arrested on a warrant rather than under suspicion of committing an offence, making attendance not necessary. These figures are again in line with Phillips and Brown's (forthcoming) findings, which showed a rise in face-to-face consultations and a decline in advice solely given by telephone. Phillips and Brown suggest that the use of legal representatives by solicitors' firms may now allow legal advice to be given at the station in more cases.[6]

---

6   Phillips and Brown compared their figures with two studies conducted in the late 1980s and early 1990s (see Sanders et al., 1989; Brown et al., 1992).

Figure 3.1 Type of legal consultation

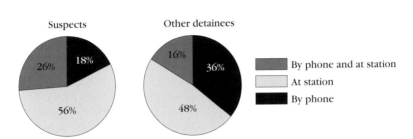

Note:
1. Sample size = 4,171 (all those receiving legal consultation).

Research by both Brown (1989) and Phillips and Brown (forthcoming) showed wide variations between stations in the way legal advice was provided, and this is also the case in the present study. In the custody record sample, over a third of suspects at Campbell Square police station received their only legal advice via the telephone, compared to six per cent of those at Peterborough. These variations are most likely to be due to local arrangements concerning the provision of legal advice (see Brown et al., 1992). Phillips and Brown (forthcoming) also raise the possibility of such variations being due to differences in the facilities available in police station custody areas. Of the 13 stations in the observation sample only two (Beaumont Leys and Campbell Square) had a telephone booth in the custody area, thereby allowing private conversations to take place between a detainee and a legal adviser. Both Gateshead and Stretford had a 'private phone' which was situated in the corner of the custody area. At the remaining stations legal consultations via the telephone occurred at the custody officer's counter or desk, leaving suspects extremely constrained in what they could discuss. The custody areas at Beaumont Leys, Campbell Square, Gateshead and Stretford all had designated rooms set aside for meetings between legal advisers and clients; however, at the remaining stations such rooms did not exist, with police interview rooms tending to be used for legal consultations.

Type of lawyer consulted and their status

In both the custody record and the observed sample six out of ten suspects who received legal advice consulted their own legal adviser, while four out of ten consulted a duty solicitor. Some criticism has surrounded the use of 'legal representatives' who may be sent to a police station after the suspect has had a telephone consultation with a solicitor.[7] The problems raised include a lack of legal expertise and confidence, the possibility of being co-opted or exploited by the police, and a failure to reveal their status to suspects (McConville and Hodgson, 1993). In an attempt to improve the quality of advice given by representatives, the Law Society introduced a scheme whereby those passing a series of tests are accredited and given a similar rights of access to suspects as qualified solicitors under the Codes of Practice (C 6.12).

The observation study examined the status of legal advisers and found that ten per cent of consultations at a police station were with an accredited representative, while 84 per cent were with a solicitor and six per cent with an unaccredited representative. Phillips and Brown's (forthcoming) study estimated that before the accreditation scheme legal representatives gave advice in about a quarter of cases. The above figures suggest that the use of these legal advisers has declined against a rise in solicitors attending police stations and the introduction of accredited representatives. Figure 3.2 presents the status of legal advisers involved in consultations at police stations. Accredited representatives were most likely to be consulted at the police station when the suspect's own legal adviser was requested. A fully qualified solicitor was most likely to advise through the duty solicitor scheme. This is because the Law Society's duty solicitor regulations limit the amount of use duty solicitors can make of representatives.

---

7   'Legal representative' refers to a range of non-solicitor staff including articled clerks, former police officers and employees of outside agencies supplying legal advice services on contract to solicitors.

Figure 3.2 Type of legal adviser by status

Note:
1. Sample size = 4,171 (all those receiving legal consultation).

Overall, since the introduction of the Law Society scheme accredited representatives now provide legal advice at police stations in a notable proportion of cases. This development is of significance since the new provisions concerning the right of silence mean that expert advice is required if a suspect is to negotiate police questioning without self-incrimination. Whether suspects are now receiving better quality advice is unclear although this issue is being addressed as part of a research project on accredited representatives funded by the Law Society.

Number and length of consultations

Legal advice given over the telephone was rarely given on more than one occasion. Of those having telephone consultations, 91 per cent had a single call, while only nine per cent had more than one. Multiple consultations were more common when a legal adviser attended the police station. A quarter of suspects had two or more consultations.

The observation research examined the length of consultations between suspects and legal advisers at police stations; one of the reasons for doing this being to see if the new provisions concerning the right of silence lengthened such meetings. Nearly half of all consultations took less than 15 minutes, while only two per cent lasted over an hour.[8]

---

8   Appendix Table A.3 outlines the length of all legal consultations.

Both the number of consultations and their length was linked to the seriousness of the offences involved, with those offences considered moderately or very serious likely to lead to multiple and lengthier consultations.[9] For example, of the ten consultations lasting over an hour, two involved murder, one GBH and one robbery.

Comparisons with previous research suggest that legal consultations *have* increased in their duration. McConville and Hodgson (1993) found that 22 per cent of legal consultations lasted less than five minutes, while the current study found only seven per cent to last this long. Forty-two per cent of consultations in McConville and Hodgson's study lasted between ten and 30 minutes, with this figure increasing to 55 per cent in the current study. Faced with changes in the right of silence legal advisers may be taking time to guide their client on how to avoid self-incrimination.

Key points

- Detainees are increasingly likely to exercise their right to legal advice while in custody. There appears to have been a steady rise in the proportion of detainees requesting legal advice, with four out of ten now doing so. A notable increase was found among juveniles who are now requesting legal advice at the same rate as adults.

- Variations were found in requests for legal advice across stations and according to sex and ethnicity.

- The main reason suspects declined legal advice was that they did not feel that it was necessary under the circumstances.

- In 11 per cent of cases requests for legal advice did not lead to its provision. The most common reasons were that suspects changed their minds, were released before a solicitor could attend, or agreed to see a solicitor in court rather than at the station. No cases were found where officers had delayed access to legal advice on the basis that it might hinder related investigations.

- Around a third of suspects and a quarter of other detainees actually received legal advice while in custody. Despite the rise in requests for advice this figure was only slightly higher than previous studies. The

---

9   Offences were categorised into three groups: very serious; moderately serious; and less serious. The offences making up each of these groups can be found in Appendix B.

vast majority of suspects who requested legal advice had at least one face-to-face consultation with a legal adviser.

- Compared to previous studies the proportion of 'legal representatives' standing in for solicitors and giving advice to suspects appears to have declined, with a corresponding rise in solicitors giving advice and the introduction of an accreditation scheme for representatives. Accredited representatives were most likely to give advice when a suspect's own legal adviser (rather than a duty solicitor) had been requested.

- Most consultations lasted no more than 15 minutes, with only one per cent lasting over an hour. In the context of previous research legal consultations appeared to have increased in length, perhaps as a result of changes to the right of silence.

4 The interviewing of suspects

This chapter examines three aspects of police interviews with suspects in custody. The first part considers the frequency of interviewing and the extent to which legal advisers are present during such encounters. The second part focuses upon the extent to which suspects make confessions during police interviews, while the third part addresses suspects' use of the right of silence. The Criminal Justice and Public Order Act 1994 (CJPOA) made important revisions to the right of silence and the impact of these is explored together with the use of 'special warnings' which can be used in relation to specific forms of evidence.

Interviews and legal advisers

Frequency of interviews

Six out of ten of all detainees in both the custody record and the observation studies were interviewed by the police during their time in custody (exactly the same figure was found by Brown et al. (1992)). The vast majority of suspects in both studies were questioned only once (90%), with only one out of ten interviewed twice or more.[1] Second interviews were even uncommon for serious crimes: just under one in five of those arrested for serious offences were interviewed more than once.

Previous studies have suggested a decline in the extent of interviewing (see Irving and McKenzie, 1989; Brown, 1989; Brown et al., 1992). Stricter access to prisoners under PACE and increasing police workloads are among some of the explanations given for this decline. The current research found the level of multiple interviewing to be broadly the same as that given by Brown et al., suggesting that the decline seen during the 1980s and early 1990s has now stabilised.

---

1   Appendix Table A.4 presents the frequency of police interviews with suspects according to offence.

Legal advisers at interviews

The presence of a legal adviser during police questioning is seen by some commentators as providing an important form of support for suspects (Sanders et al., 1989). More specifically, research has suggested that suspects are more likely to exercise the right of silence when a legal adviser is present; this may be due to advice given or more general support gained from the adviser's presence (Sanders et al., 1989; Moston et al, 1990).

Figure 4.1 Extent of legal advice for suspects interviewed by police officers

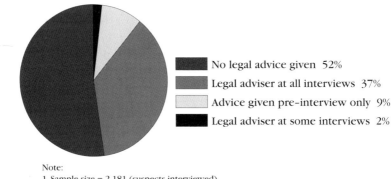

Note:
1. Sample size = 2,181 (suspects interviewed).

Figure 4.1 shows the extent of legal advice received by those suspects interviewed while in custody. In general, just under half of all suspects interviewed received some form of legal advice. Over a third of suspects had a legal adviser present during all police interviews, an additional two per cent had a legal adviser present at some interviews, and nine per cent received legal advice only prior to an interview. In just over half of cases no legal advice was received either prior to the interview or during it.

The likelihood of legal advisers attending all interviews varied widely; from eight per cent at Campbell Square to 53 per cent at Hackney[2]. Such variations tended to be linked partly to the provision of pre-interview advice. Where the proportion of legal advisers attending interviews was particularly low, the provision of pre-interview advice tended to be high (most notably in the cases of Campbell Square, Luton and Southampton). The proportion of

2   Appendix Table A.5 presents figures for legal advice received by suspects for each station.

suspects not seeking legal advice, either before or during police questioning, varied from 41 per cent (Hackney) to 65 per cent (Gateshead). Not surprisingly, another factor linked with variations was the seriousness of the offence involved; seven out of ten suspects arrested for serious offences had a legal adviser present during all police questioning, compared to a quarter of those arrested for less serious offences.

Comparison with previous studies indicates a pronounced rise in legal advisers attending police interviews. Brown (1989) found that legal advisers attended all police interviews in only 12 per cent of cases - one-third the level found in the current study. This large increase in attendance is only partly due to the rise in requests for legal advice, with a more useful way of looking at this issue being to consider the rate legal advisers attend interview in legal advice cases only. Again these figures indicate a rise, although a more modest one. Sanders et al. (1989) found that a legal adviser attended at least one interview in two-thirds of cases in which advice was provided, while in the present study the corresponding figure was 75 per cent. When Sanders et al. excluded telephone consultations, legal advisers attended police interviews in 81 per cent of cases in which they consulted with their clients at the police station, while in the current study that figure was 91 per cent.

One explanation for this increase concerns the changes to the right of silence. It is reasonable to suggest that legal advisers are now more likely to decide that their presence is required during interviews in order to steer their clients through police questioning. The extent to which suspects make damaging admissions during police questioning is examined in the next section.

Confessions

Various studies have found that at least half of suspects in detention confess when questioned by officers (see Sanders et al., 1989; McConville, 1993; Moston and Stephenson, 1993). This was also the case in the interviewing officer sample which found confessions were made by 58 per cent of suspects. This figure is comprised of those who confessed to all offences for which they had been arrested (45%), and those who confessed to only some offences (13%).

The likelihood of confessions being made varied between groups of suspects. Women were more likely to make admissions than men (65 and 56% respectively), and juveniles more likely than adults (65 and 55% respectively). In terms of ethnicity, a higher proportion of whites made confessions (60%) compared to Afro-Caribbean and Asians (48 and 51% respectively). Rather than these variations reflecting other factors, statistical analysis has found both ethnicity and sex to be significant predictors of confessions (see Phillips and Brown, forthcoming). Legal advice has commonly been seen as an important influence on whether confessions are made, with a number of studies showing the confession rate to be lower where suspects receive advice (see Sanders et al., 1989; Moston and Stephenson, 1993; Phillips and Brown, forthcoming). This was also the case in the present study, where 47 per cent of suspects receiving legal advice prior to interview made confessions, compared to 66 per cent of those receiving no advice.[3]

Four per cent of suspects confessed to offences other than those for which they were arrested. It is unclear whether these offences were committed at another time, or on the same occasion as that for which the suspect had been arrested. However almost all those making such admissions had been arrested for offences involving either burglary, shoplifting and thefts concerning motor vehicles. Such offences are especially likely to be repeat offences, so it is likely that officers would question suspects about other possible incidents.

Comparison with research conducted just before the introduction of the revised Codes of Practice and the new provisions concerning the right of silence suggests that confessions have remained at broadly the same level (current research: 58%; Philips and Brown: 55%). Whether the provisions concerning the right of silence have had any other form of impact is examined in the next section.

The right of silence

The new provisions concerning the right of silence have been one of the highest profile developments in criminal justice over recent years. Under the CJPOA, courts are now allowed to draw such inferences as appear proper from a person's use of the right of silence. These inferences can be drawn in four circumstances. The first is when a defendant uses a defence in court which they failed to mention earlier when questioned or charged by the police (s34). The second is when a defendant aged 14 years or over refuses to give evidence at trial (s35). The third and fourth are when a suspect, having been issued with a 'special warning' under the Act, fails to account for incriminating objects, marks or substances (s36) or for their presence at a particular place (s37). An important issue is whether sections 34, 36 and 37 have had any effect on the extent to which suspects use the right of silence during police interviews.[4]

---

3   Brown (1997) suggests in his review of research on PACE that advice given by legal advisers prior to interview is mainly in line with the suspect's inclinations. For Brown, this suggests that the provision of legal advice to suspects may not, by itself, have had a significant impact on confessions.

4   A fuller account of these findings will be published in the future, together with other research exploring the impact of this legislation.

The use of the right of silence under the new provisions

Studies undertaken before the new provisions provided estimates on the use of the right of silence ranging from six per cent (Leng, 1993) to 23 per cent (Phillips and Brown, forthcoming). Explanations for such disparities tend to focus upon differences in the definition of silence and in sampling methods (see Brown, 1997; Leng, 1994). Brown (1994) in a review of research for the RCCJ suggests that 10 per cent of suspects outside the Metropolitan Police exercise their right of silence, with the proportion rising to around 16 per cent in London. These estimates include both suspects who refuse to answer all questions and those who answer questions selectively. In updating his review, Brown (1997) raises the possibility that an increase in the use of the right of silence may have occurred during the early 1990s but prior to the CJPOA. This is based on Phillips and Brown's work and on an ACPO study (1993) which found ten per cent of suspects refusing to answer all questions and 12 per cent refusing to answer some.[5] Brown suggests that such a rise may be due to increases in the provision of legal advice and a greater awareness of the right of silence due to media attention given to miscarriages of justice, the creation and reporting of the RCCJ and government proposals to change the law in this area.

A specific comparison of suspects' use of the right of silence before and after the introduction of the new provisions is possible with reference to an earlier piece of research. Phillips and Brown's study, conducted prior to the new provisions, and the current research, conducted after their introduction, included fieldwork at the same eight stations using the same methodology.[6] Table 4.1 presents figures from each study for the eight police stations. A comparison of the figures indicates a notable reduction in suspects using the right of silence. In Phillips and Brown's study ten per cent of suspects gave 'no comment' interviews by refusing all questions from officers; in the current study this figure had fallen to six per cent. Thirteen per cent of suspects selectively answered police questions in Phillips and Brown's study, while in the current study this fell to ten per cent. There has been a consequent rise in suspects answering all questions. Suspects were found to be less likely to exercise the right of silence across all stations. Furthermore, reductions in the use of silence were found to be greatest among suspects receiving legal advice. This may be a result of legal advisers warning their clients about the consequences of remaining silent under the new provisions.

---

5   Brown (1997) notes that a lack of information concerning the methodology used in the ACPO study means that it is difficult to assess the validity of the resulting figures.

6   The stations were Beaumont Leys, Croydon, Gateshead, Hackney, Luton, Queens Road, Rochdale, Stretford. Both studies gave interviewing officers a self-completion questionnaire.

Table 4.1 Suspects' use of the right of silence by study

Study	Refused all questions %	Refused some questions %	Answered all questions %
Phillips and Brown	10	13	77
Current study	6	10	84

Note:
1. Sample sizes (suspects interviewed in the eight stations): Phillips and Brown=1,785; current study=1,227.

Suspects' use of silence was linked to seriousness of offence. Fourteen per cent of suspects arrested for serious offences gave 'no comment' interviews, compared to seven per cent arrested for moderately serious offences and three per cent arrested for less serious offences. Afro-Caribbean suspects were more likely to exercise their right of silence, compared to other ethnic groups: 12 per cent of Afro-Caribbeans refused to answer some questions, against nine per cent of whites and eight per cent of Asians; seven per cent of Afro-Caribbeans refused all questions, against five per cent of whites and six per cent of Asians. These differences were statistically significant. Offence profiles do not seem to explain these differences, with few ethnic variations found in terms of seriousness and type of offence. Men were more likely to exercise their right of silence compared to women, with ten per cent (refusing selected) questions compared to seven per cent of women, and six per cent giving 'no comment' interviews compared to three per cent of women. No differences were found between adults and juveniles.

Commentators have emphasised the need to be clear about the kinds of questions suspects actually refuse to answer as not all silences may be incriminating, especially if they relate to others' involvement in the offence (Leng, 1994). Table 4.2 relates to those suspects who answered questions selectively for all 13 stations in the investigating officer sample. Suspects were almost as likely to refuse questions concerning other people's involvement in an offence as those relating to their own involvement. This suggests that some suspects may use silence so as not to implicate others rather than to protect themselves. Under the new provisions inferences could not be drawn in these circumstances. Overall, the great majority of refusals concerned the suspect's or someone else's involvement with an offence; questions unrelated to the offence appear rarely to be refused.

Table 4.2 Selective responses to questioning: type of questions refused

Type of question refused	%
About own involvement in offence only	48
Others' involvement in offence only	46
Questions not related to offence	6

Note:
1. Sample size= 314 (suspects refusing some questions).

The use of special warnings

Under the 'special warnings' provisions of the CJPOA, inferences may in certain circumstances be drawn from a suspect's failure to answer police questions about incriminating circumstances. Unlike s34 these provisions do not require a defence to be raised at court which had not been raised earlier. The failure to provide a satisfactory account at the time of interview is enough to allow inferences to be drawn. The new provisions relate to cases where a suspect interviewed after arrest fails to account for incriminating objects, marks or substances (s36) or his or her presence at a particular place (s37). For example, in a case of violent assault officers may wish to question a suspect about their cut hands or torn clothing; or in a case of criminal damage a suspect may be asked what he or she was doing outside a shop at about the time its windows were broken. In order for inferences to be drawn later at court, the Codes of Practice stipulate that the interviewing officer must give the suspect what is termed a 'special warning' (C 10.5B and E 4.3D). Such a warning requires officers to explain the following to the suspect:

i) the offence being investigated;

ii) what fact the suspect is being asked to account for;

iii) the officer's belief that the fact may be due to the suspect's participation in the commission of that offence;

iv) that a court may draw proper inferences if a suspect fails or refuses to account for that fact;

v) that a record is being made of the interview and it may given in evidence if the suspect is brought to trial.

Thirty-nine per cent of suspects exercising silence were given either a s36 or s37 special warning (7% of all suspects interviewed). These were spread over a range of different offences, with similar proportions of those arrested for burglary (11%), violence (7%), drugs (7%) and robbery (6%) given warnings. In some cases officers may have administered a special warning before then raising the subject of marks or a suspect's presence at a crime scene, in others the suspect may have already refused to answer such questions. Under both these circumstances the suspect will have had an opportunity to answer specific questions having been given a special warning. Table 4.3 shows how suspects responded to special warnings. It is clear the majority refused to provide an account (s36: 70%; s37: 77%) or gave one which was considered unsatisfactory by officers (s36: 11%; s37: 10%). In a relatively small proportion of cases a special warning resulted in a satisfactory account being given (s36: 19%; s37: 13%). However, since these special warnings were created in order to provide additional evidence in any later proceedings, their effectiveness should not be measured purely against their ability to encourage suspects to provide accounts during police questioning.

Table 4.3 Result of s36 and s37 special warnings

	s36 special warnings (marks, objects, substances)	s37 special warning (presence at scene)
	%	%
No account given	70	77
Unsatisfactory account given	11	10
Satisfactory account given	19	13

Note:
1. Sample size=176 suspects given s36 special warning; 134 suspects given s37 special warning.

Key points

- Six out of ten detainees in both the custody record and observation studies were interviewed by police officers during their time in custody. Only ten per cent were interviewed more than once.

- Just under half of all suspects interviewed received legal advice while in custody, with legal advisers present during all interviews in 37 per cent of cases, during some interviews in two per cent of cases and providing advice before an interview only in nine per cent.

- The rate at which legal advisers attended police interviews has risen compared to previous studies. In 75 per cent of cases where legal advice had been given, a legal adviser attended all or some police interviews.

- Fifty-eight per cent of all suspects made confessions while in police custody. The proportion of suspects making confessions appears to have remained at the same level as before the revised Codes of Practice and the new provisions relating to the right of silence were introduced.

- Comparison with past research indicates a significant reduction in the use of the right of silence. Suspects were found to be less likely to give complete 'no comment' interviews or refuse questions selectively.

- Silence is commonly used not only to protect the suspect but to avoid implicating others.

- Five per cent of all suspects were given either a s36 or s37 special warning, with relatively small proportions then going on to give satisfactory accounts.

5 Identification and investigation procedures

This chapter examines the taking of samples from detainees for forensic analysis, the searching of suspects, and the use of photographs and identification parades. A brief description of each set of powers and any related changes in the Codes of Practice is followed by findings from the custody record and observation studies.

Forensic analysis and DNA profiling

Since the late 1980s DNA profiling has helped the police to establish a suspect's guilt or innocence in certain criminal cases. This is possible because each individual's DNA profile is unique, thereby allowing a scientific test to compare, for example, a semen stain recovered from a crime scene with a suspect's blood sample. Following the success of this new technique, a national DNA database became operational and DNA profiles are now used to search across the database against other samples from undetected crimes. A match made during such a search may implicate a suspect in a previously undetected crime. The database also allows samples from a crime scene to be searched against existing records on the database in case the perpetrator has already given a sample, or for samples from unsolved cases to be placed on the database for future reference. Safeguards mean that the database only contains profiles of suspects charged with or reported for recordable offences,[1] while individuals no longer suspected of a crime have their profiles removed from the database.

Samples taken from suspects for forensic analysis are divided according to whether they are 'non-intimate' or 'intimate'. The following sections define these terms, outline the changes in the Codes of Practice concerning sampling, and examine the extent and nature of sampling in relation to suspects in custody.

---

1   Recordable offences include all imprisonable offences and a number of specified non-imprisonable offences.

Non-intimate samples

Non-intimate samples can be taken without a suspect's consent and are defined by the Codes of Practice (D 5.11) to include:

- a sample of hair (other than pubic hair)

- a sample taken from a nail or from under a nail

- a swab taken from any part of a person's body including the mouth but not any other body orifice

- saliva

- a footprint or similar impression of any part of a person's body other than the hand.

The Codes of Practice make three important alterations to the taking of these samples. The first addresses samples taken from inside the mouth which were previously defined as 'intimate samples' and required a suspect's consent. Saliva and mouth swabs are now defined as non-intimate samples and can therefore be taken when a suspect refuses to provide such a specimen. The objective of this change is to ensure that suitable samples for DNA profiling can be taken from suspects when officers believe it is necessary.

In a second alteration the Code allows non-intimate samples to be taken for recordable offences rather than, as in the past, serious arrestable offences (D 5.5). This greatly expands the range of offences where samples can be secured and goes beyond the RCCJ recommendation that sampling should be expanded to include burglary and assault (see Steventon, 1995; Tain, 1994). A third alteration expands the circumstances in which non-intimate samples may be taken, allowing officers now to take samples from persons who have been charged with or informed that they will be reported for a recordable offence, and from persons convicted of a recordable offence (D 5.5). This power extends sampling to those cases where DNA evidence has not been a relevant factor in establishing guilt and permits samples to be taken from a large number of people in order to build up the DNA database.

Non-intimate samples were taken from seven per cent of suspects in the custody record sample in connection with a wide range of offences, including theft, criminal damage, drugs and public disorder. Initially this range of offences suggests some divergence from the official policies of police forces involved in the study. These policies, in line with ACPO (1995) and Home Office guidance (1995), advise that samples should only be taken from detainees suspected of the following crimes:

- offences against the person

- sexual offences

- burglaries.

One explanation for the sampling of other offences is that these were taken if the case involved a persistent offender who had a history of more serious crimes. Therefore, someone charged with theft, or a public order offence, may be sampled because they had previously been convicted of a burglary, or a violent crime. This is confirmed by other research which found that the policy guidelines of various police forces encouraged officers to take 'intelligence-led' samples from those *suspected* of crimes in the designated categories, even if they had been arrested for another type of offence (Morgan, et al., 1996).

In light of this policy Figure 5.1 outlines the level of sampling within each offence group. The table shows that the most common offences for which samples were taken were those designated by the Home Office and ACPO, but that sampling did occur for other offences even if this was at a much lower level. Sampling was most common in connection with sexual offences (25%), with around a third of those arrested for rape and over half arrested for gross indecency with a child providing samples. Samples were also often taken from those charged with acts of violence, burglary and robbery; however a clear distinction can be seen in the level of sampling for these offences and the remaining groups. The level of sampling in the target categories is still relatively low, with this being partly dependent on the availability of other evidence, such as a suspect's confession or eye witnesses' statements.

Figure 5.1 Non-intimate samples taken within each offence group

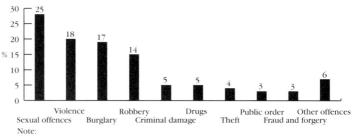

Note:
1. Sample size = 758 (suspects providing non–intimate samples).

Just over half of those in the custody record research gave their consent to a non-intimate sample. The Codes of Practice do not require officers to record what kind of sample was taken, however Figure 5.2 details the kinds of sample when a description was given. In the vast majority of cases swabs were taken from the mouth or body, while other forms of sampling were very rare. This broadly confirms discussions with custody officers who stated that mouth swabs were the preferred method of taking a sample, despite hair, when plucked by the root, apparently being much better for DNA analysis. This preference hinged on only two mouth swabs being required for an non-intimate sample, compared to ten separate hairs. The relative ease of taking a mouth swab and lack of pain meant that officers would normally decide on this kind of sample in the first instance, only taking hair samples when a suspect's refusal made taking a swab difficult.

Figure 5.2 Type of non-intimate sample taken

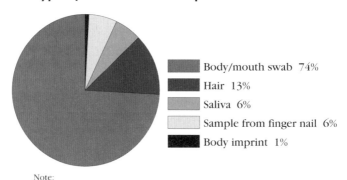

Note:
1. Sample size = 242 (cases where type of non–imtimate sample known).

Figure 5.3 shows that the majority of non-intimate samples were taken to provide a record after the suspect had been charged, while a much smaller proportion were taken in order to ascertain a suspect's involvement in an offence. In those cases where officers had enough evidence to charge, any samples taken would be used to build up the national DNA database. The taking of mouth swabs from suspects without consent was the subject of some concern as the CJPOA passed through parliament. While the custody record sample did not differentiate between mouth and body swabs, 10 per cent of these samples were taken without consent. These cases covered a broad range of offences, however the majority involved either violence, theft or burglary.

Figure 5.3 Grounds for taking non-intimate sample

Suspect to be charged. Samples required 82%

To ascertain involvement in offence(s) 18%

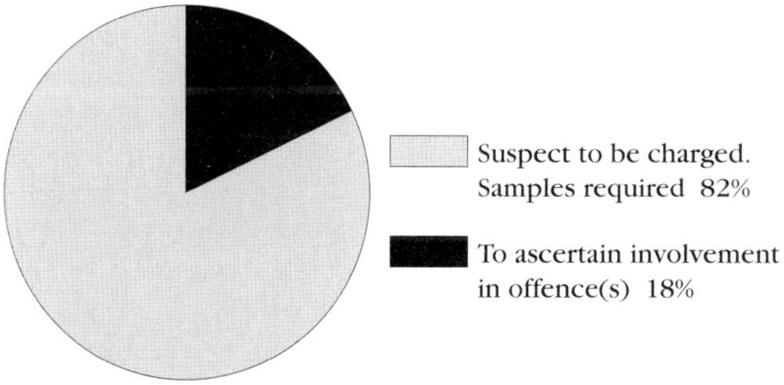

Note:
1. Sample size = 758 (all suspects providing non-intimate samples).

Before obtaining a sample the Codes of Practice require officers to tell a suspect the grounds for taking it (D 5.11B). Few suspects in the observation sample asked for any further explanation (8%), two per cent were described as abusive or annoyed, while the vast majority did not respond (90%). Non-intimate samples were nearly always taken by the officer in the case, in most cases at the same time as the suspect was being photographed and fingerprinted.[2] Under these circumstances one or two officers and the suspect were usually the only people involved in sampling, with a police surgeon or an appropriate adult present in a very small proportion of cases (both 2%).

---

2   At one station a lack of training meant that custody officers took samples.

Intimate samples

The Codes of Practice (D 5.11) define intimate samples as including

- dental impressions

- samples of blood, semen or any other tissue fluid

- urine

- pubic hair

- swabs taken from a person's body orifice other than the mouth.

As with non-intimate samples, these can now be taken in connection with recordable offences (D 5.1). Intimate samples were taken very rarely.[3] Only 40 out of 10,496 suspects in the custody record sample provided such samples (well under one per cent of all suspects) with these being taken in cases involving serious crimes against the person such as murder, rape and robbery. Intimate samples require the authorisation of an officer of at least superintendent rank *and* the consent of the suspect (D 5.1). If a person refuses to provide such a sample they can be warned under s62 of PACE that this refusal may harm their case if it goes to trial (D 5.2). Twenty-three suspects were given what is called a 's62 warning', three of whom still refused to provide a sample; these suspects had been arrested for, robbery, possession of controlled drugs and violent disorder.[4]

Figure 5.4 shows the different types of intimate sample taken, with blood being the most common. Blood and non-specified samples were taken mainly for offences concerning acts of violence, robbery and sexual offences, while, not surprisingly, samples of semen, pubic hair and swabs from body orifices related to sexual offences.

---

3   An additional 94 people gave samples of blood or urine which did not fall under 'intimate samples' since these detainees had been arrested in connection with drink driving offences and gave samples under the Road Traffic Act.

4   Two of these were later charged and detained, while the suspect arrested for violent disorder was bailed for police enquiries.

Figure 5.4 Type of intimate sample taken

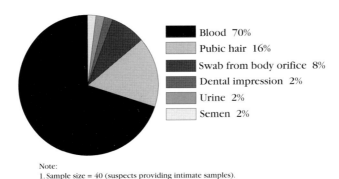

Blood 70%
Pubic hair 16%
Swab from body orifice 8%
Dental impression 2%
Urine 2%
Semen 2%

Note:
1. Sample size = 40 (suspects providing intimate samples).

The observation research found the taking of intimate samples to be as rare as the custody record study, with all of the suspects concerned providing no response to being informed that the police wished to take a sample. A police surgeon or dentist took all the samples while police officers were present in half of the cases.

Body searches

Most people entering detention will face some form of non-intimate search, including an inspection of their pockets and a 'frisk' by officers, before being placed in a cell (C 4.1). In addition, some suspects may be given a strip search, during which more than outer clothing is removed, or an intimate search, involving an examination of a person's body orifices other than the mouth. In the past an intimate search included the examination of the mouth. However, this caused problems in cases where a suspect used the mouth to conceal evidence, such as controlled drugs, and an arresting officer was not lawfully able to recover evidence without seeking authorisation for an intimate search. A search of the mouth is now defined as a non-intimate search which can be conducted on arrest if the officer has reasonable grounds to believe the suspect is concealing evidence, or later at the police station. However, the taking of a dental impression would require a dentist as this is classified as an intimate sample.

Strip searches

Strip searches are conducted when officers have reasonable grounds to believe a suspect may be concealing an article while in detention (Code C, Annex A). Three per cent of suspects were strip-searched in the custody record sample. By far the most common group to undergo such a search were those arrested for drug offences, with just under a quarter of this group being searched. The frequency of strip searches varied between forces with seven per cent of suspects strip-searched in the Metropolitan Police compared to one per cent in the majority of other forces. Figure 5.5 shows the items being sought during the strip search. As might be expected in the light of the high number of drug related offences involved, the majority of searches were for controlled substances, while other searches related to concealed weapons and stolen goods. Strip searches resulted in a relatively low success rate, with items found in only 12 per cent of cases. Controlled drugs (7%) were the most common items uncovered, with stolen goods (1%) and knives and other weapons (1%) found in a small number of cases. Searches also revealed additional items (3%) which were either related to the arrest, such as a crack pipe, or could be used to cause harm or damage, such as a cigarette lighter.

Figure 5.5 Grounds for strip search

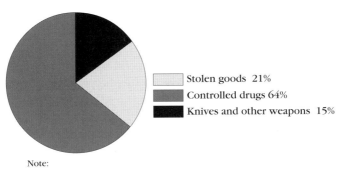

Stolen goods 21%
Controlled drugs 64%
Knives and other weapons 15%

Note:
1. Sample size = 275 (suspects strip searched).

In the observation sample few suspects responded when informed that a strip search was to be carried out. The majority simply consented (80%), with only a small proportion asking for an explanation (4%), and the remainder described as being either annoyed or abusive (16%). The Codes of Practice require that only those who need to be present should be involved in strip searching a suspect. This usually meant one or two officers conducting the search by themselves, while only three per cent of cases involved an appropriate adult or doctor.

Intimate searches

An intimate search may only be conducted if an officer of the rank of superintendent or above has reasonable grounds for believing the suspect is either concealing an article which could harm that person or others at the police station, or is concealing a Class A drug with intent to supply or export (Code C, Annex A). The actual physical examination under normal circumstances should be conducted by a doctor.

Intimate searches were carried out on only 17 out of 10,496 suspects in the custody record sample. These suspects had been arrested either for violent acquisitive crimes, such as aggravated burglary and robbery, or drug offences. The decision to make such a search might be based on the nature of the arrest (for example, if it involved the possession of Class A drugs), or on police records and knowledge about previous offences. Little information was recorded about the results of these searches, but the parts of the body inspected were listed and included the nose, ears, anal passage and vaginal passage.

Photographs and ID parades

A photograph of a person in custody can be taken either with their consent (D 4.1), or without it under the following circumstances (D 4.2):

- When the suspect is arrested with others and a photograph would establish who was arrested at what place and at what time;

- When the suspect has been charged with or reported for a recordable offence and has not yet been released or brought before a court;

- When the suspect has been convicted of a recordable offence and his photograph is not already on record; or

- If an officer of at least the rank of superintendent authorises it, having reasonable grounds for suspecting the involvement of that person in a criminal offence where identification evidence is available.

Forty-one per cent of suspects had their photographs taken while in custody and the vast majority of these had been charged or bailed. Only ten people had their photograph taken without their consent (less than one per cent of all suspects photographed). Those not giving their consent had been arrested for theft, ABH, burglary, robbery or possession of an offensive weapon, and while most were charged at the end of their detention, two were photographed and bailed pending an identification parade.

When suspects are bailed pending an identification procedure, they may be told that any attempt to alter their appearance between release from police custody and the future identification procedure may be given in evidence if a case goes to court (D 4.1). In the observation sample four per cent of those bailed were bailed pending an identification parade. These people were most likely to be suspected of violent offences, followed by thefts and robberies. Half of those bailed for a parade were warned about the consequences of changing their appearance, with robbery suspects being the most likely to be warned.

Interviews with inspectors responsible for identification procedures at various police stations indicated that in a small number of cases suspects did attempt to change their appearance prior to a parade. One officer estimated the proportion to be about five per cent of suspects, with changes involving shaven heads, beards, moustaches and dyed hair. It was unclear just how many parades did not go ahead due to changes in a suspect's appearance, since officers tried to circumvent any problems. Measures included persuading the suspect to shave off a beard, or wear a hat, or using a different identification procedure such as confronting the suspect with the witness. At least one of the above strategies might be used before the suspect was reported as obstructing the identification procedure.

Photographs of suspects, either taken at the time of arrest or before being bailed, were viewed as important in establishing a change of appearance and in negotiating to have facial hair removed. Photographs also avoided errors with, for example, written descriptions of a suspect sometimes leading to inappropriate volunteers being selected for a parade. However, warning a suspect about the consequences of changing his or her appearance was not viewed as a deterrent, with some stating that the suspect had little to lose by making such alterations. In such cases establishing that a change of appearance had been made was viewed as a relatively weak piece of evidence compared to a positive identification by a witness. In short, suspects had more to gain than lose in changing their appearance, with some officers suggesting that stronger sanctions should exist, such as a presumption of guilt or adverse inferences. In a wider context, officers estimated that 20 to 30 per cent of identification procedures did not go ahead, with the main reason given being that suspects and witnesses simply failed to appear for the procedure.

Key points

- Non-intimate samples were taken in a very small proportion of cases (7%), which usually involved violence against the person, sexual offences or burglary. The majority of suspects providing non-intimate samples gave their consent. Samples were mainly taken to provide a record for future investigations, and were most commonly taken using a mouth swab.

- Intimate samples were taken in less than one per cent of cases, usually in serious offences such as murder, rape and robbery. Blood was by far the most common form of intimate sample taken.

- Three per cent of suspects were strip searched, with over half of these having been arrested in relation to supplying or possessing controlled drugs. Around one search in eight led to any items being found.

- Less than one per cent of suspects were given an intimate search. Such searches were connected to violent acquisitive crimes, such as aggravated burglary and robbery, or drug offences.

- Very few suspects refused or questioned police requests for a sample or a search.

- Four out of ten suspects were photographed while in custody, with less than one per cent of these being photographed without their consent. In a small number of cases those bailed pending an identification parade were found to have changed their appearance prior to the parade. Faced with such behaviour officers tended to use various strategies to circumvent any changes. Suspects and witnesses failing to appear, rather than any changes in a suspect's appearance, were said to be a greater factor in the failure of identification procedures.

6 Disposal decisions

This chapter examines what happens to suspects at the end of their time in police detention.[1] The outcome of police detention is examined according to type of offence, the station at which the case was dealt with, and the age of the detainee. In some instances officers deferred the final decision about a case by bailing or reporting a suspect for summons, meaning that a final decision was not made until after the end of the research. However, it was possible to make projections about the outcome of those cases in which the final decision was deferred.

Outcome of cases

There are three main options facing the custody officer when a suspect's detention is no longer justified. If there is sufficient evidence the officer may charge the suspect or, in less serious cases where the suspect has admitted the offence, administer a caution. The second option involves the police releasing the suspect and closing the case with no further action (NFA). This occurs when officers find no evidence against a suspect or where evidence *does* exist but officers decide that charging would serve no useful purpose. The third option is to delay making a decision. Here officers may want more time in order to make further enquiries, may want to arrange an identification parade, or may be satisfied about a suspect's involvement in an offence, but may be unsure whether to proceed with a charge. In these cases the suspect might be bailed to return to the station on a specific date, or may be told that the facts of the case will be reported with a view to prosecution and that they may receive a summons.

Outcome by offence

Traditionally, adult and juvenile suspects have been treated differently. In particular, diversion from prosecution has been seen as a common measure for juveniles who may not come to the police's attention again. Adults and juveniles are therefore treated separately in the following discussion. Table

---

1   The Codes of Practice state that when officers believe enough evidence is available to prosecute a suspect the case should be immediately brought before a custody officer, who is then responsible for considering whether or not the detainee should be charged (C 16.1).

6.1 presents figures from the custody record sample on the outcome of detention for adults by seriousness of offence. Over six out of ten adults had some form of official action taken against them at the end of their time in custody: 52 per cent were charged, while 11 per cent were cautioned. Over a fifth had decision about their case deferred either through reporting for summons (12%) or through bail (10%), while 19 per cent had their case NFAed. A small proportion fell into the 'other' category (6%), which included cases where, for example, the suspect was transferred to another police station, returned to prison or taken to hospital.

Table 6.1 Outcome of detention according to seriousness of offence (adult suspects)

Outcome	Serious offences	Moderate offences	Minor offences	All offences
	%	%	%	%
Charge	58	55	46	52
Instant caution	3	9	17	11
Summons	•	2	3	2
Bail	15	12	3	10
NFA	14	17	22	19
Other	10	5	9	6
Total	100	100	100	100

Notes:
1. Table does not contain outcome of detention for juvenile suspects.
2. Sample size= 8,160 (adult suspects).
3. •=less than one per cent.

Nearly 60 per cent of those arrested for serious offences were charged before leaving custody, compared to under half of those arrested for minor offences. Cautions were more likely to be used for minor offences (17%), compared to moderate and serious offences (9 and 3%, respectively). Decisions were most likely to be deferred for serious and moderately serious offences. Over one in five suspects arrested for minor offences were released unconditionally; some of these received informal warnings. Unconditional releases were less likely for suspects arrested for serious or moderate offences (14 and 17%, respectively).

Compared to Brown's study (1989), the proportion of suspects charged for minor offences has strongly declined while staying broadly the same for moderate and serious offences. Brown found 61 per cent of suspects arrested for minor offences were charged, compared to 46 per cent in the current study. In this light one might expect the level of cautions for minor offences to have risen, yet they remain at about the same level. While the disparity is partly due to slightly more suspects being bailed or summonsed in Brown's study, the main difference concerns suspects being given unconditional releases. In Brown's study six per cent of suspects arrested for minor offences were NFAed, while in the current study that figure was nearly four times greater (22%). Similar changes are also reflected in official criminal statistics concerning police clear-ups for all offences. These show a decline in charging since 1989 and a rise in clear-ups by 'other' means (Home Office, 1996). Such clear-ups would be contained within the category of NFAs as the outcome of detention, although by no means comprising all of the category. Why these developments have occurred is unclear, but it may be due to changes in how forces are dealing with certain forms of crime, such as minor cases of criminal damage. Officers may be increasingly NFAing these crimes, perhaps issuing an informal warning, and recording the case as 'cleared up', rather than charging the suspect.

Variations across stations

The proportion of suspects charged ranged from 34 per cent (Croydon) to 68 per cent (Radford Road), while those bailed ranged from two per cent (Basingstoke) to 21 per cent (Queens Road). Variations in the proportion of suspects cautioned were less pronounced, ranging from five per cent (Beaumont Leys) to 17 per cent (Newcastle East).[2]

Variation in the disposal of cases is partly the product of different practices between stations and forces. Those arrested for drunkenness in Northumbria tended to be either charged or cautioned, while in the Metropolitan Police these cases tended to be NFAed following a warning. Hampshire, compared to other forces, was more likely to report suspects for summons, particularly in cases involving theft or criminal damage. Officers at some stations explained that they would regularly bail suspects who were unlikely to be charged as this provided an opportunity to take fingerprints and have them checked against police records. More generally, Evans and Ellis (1996) suggest that certain forces traditionally rely on certain forms of disposal more than others (for example, cautioning).

---

2   Appendix A Tables A.6 and A.7 present disposals for adult suspects for all stations and forces in the custody record sample.

55

Variations between stations are also the result of differences in the kinds of offences found there. For example, the variation in charge rates between the two Cambridgeshire stations was partly due to an above average number of arrests for minor offences at one station. Overall though, variations between stations in each force are remarkably small.

Compared to Brown's study (1989) a number of differences are noticeable. First, while cautions as a proportion of disposals have risen slightly, the variation between forces was far less in the current study. In Brown's study the proportion of suspects cautioned ranged from one to 19 per cent, while in the present study the range was from six to 15 per cent. Second, the reporting of suspects for summons appears to have greatly reduced. In Brown's study 10 per cent of all suspects were reported, with this rising to 30 per cent in one force, while in the current study this occurred for only two per cent of suspects. This change will largely be due to the police now being able to deal with the majority of drink drive cases without having to wait for the analysis of blood or urine samples.

Disposals for juveniles

Table 6.2 shows how juveniles were disposed of compared with adult suspects. They were less likely to be charged and more likely to either be cautioned, reported for summons, bailed or unconditionally released. Officers were almost twice as likely to defer a decision on juveniles compared to adults through the use of bail or by reporting for summons. Forces generally had arrangements whereby young people could be referred, via a specialised section within the force, to an inter-agency juvenile panel. The panel will consider the details of the case and recommend a course of action, which may be to charge, caution, NFA or refer the juvenile to a diversionary scheme. In Phillips and Brown's (forthcoming) study ten per cent of cases involving juveniles were eventually referred to a juvenile panel, compared to six per cent in the present study. These were mainly offences of moderate seriousness, with property crime and especially shoplifting being very common. Where the result of a referral to a juvenile panel was recorded in the custody record, 19 per cent led to a NFA, 28 per cent to a caution and 53 per cent to a charge. In a significant number of cases the decision to take no further action was accompanied by a written or verbal warning.

Table 6.2 Outcome of detention for juvenile and adult suspects

Outcome	Juveniles	17 years and above	All
	%	%	%
Charge	33	52	48
Instant caution	19	11	13
Summons	5	2	3
Bail	16	10	11
NFA	24	19	20
Other	3	6	5
Total	100	100	100

Note:
1. Sample size= juvenile suspects: 2,135; adult suspects: 8,160; all: 10,295.

The custody record sample revealed important changes in the disposal of juvenile suspects. In Brown's study (1989), 18 per cent of juvenile suspects were charged at the end of detention, while in the custody record sample this figure was almost twice as high (33%). Interestingly, instant cautions remained at about the same level (custody record sample: 19%; Brown: 20%). The major change that has occured was in the extent to which decisions were deferred or unconditional release granted. Forty-five per cent of juvenile suspects were either reported for summons or bailed in Brown's study, while the corresponding figure in the present study was only 21 per cent. Fourteen per cent of juvenile suspects were unconditionally released in Brown's study, while in the present study the figure was 24 per cent. Overall, the outcome of cases involving juvenile suspects was far more likely to be decided at the end of detention without referral elsewhere.

Despite this general pattern, wide variations were found when forces were compared.[3] These will be partly due to differences in the profile of offences and arrest practices across the forces (see Brown, 1989). In addition some forces clearly had strong policies of diverting juveniles away from prosecution. This was most clearly seen in Hampshire and Northamptonshire where large proportions of juvenile cases were dealt either through the use of summons or no further action, with the latter form of disposal involving in many cases an informal warning. Previous research

---

3   Appendix A Table A.8 presents the disposal of juveniles for each force.

indicates that these policies had existed within these forces for a long period of time (see Brown, 1989; Evans and Ellis, 1996).

Projected outcomes

Neither the custody record nor the observation sample was able to follow through cases in which suspects were summonsed or bailed.[4] However, in a significant proportion of cases involving bail or a summons the final outcome was established, allowing predictions to be made about the cases where the final disposal was not known. Table 6.3 shows the result of such a projection for juveniles and adults. Over half of all suspects were charged, while just under a quarter were NFAed. In terms of differences between adults and juveniles, 56 per cent of adults were charged compared to 40 per cent of juveniles, while over a quarter of juveniles were cautioned compared to 12 per cent of adults. When decisions to charge or caution are grouped together, around two-thirds of cases involving juveniles or adults eventually involved some form of official action. In all, 19 per cent of all cases led to the police taking no further action, while 13 per cent of cases involved some other form of outcome.

Table 6.3 Projected outcome of cases involving juvenile and adult suspects

Outcome	Juveniles	17 years and above	All
	%	%	%
Charge	40	56	53
Caution (instant/deferred)	26	12	15
NFA	19	19	19
Other	15	13	13
Total	100	100	100

Note:
1. Sample size= juvenile suspects: 2,135; adult suspects: 8,160; all 10,295.

---

4   The final disposal was not known for 15 per cent of cases in the custody record sample.

Compared to previous studies these figures indicate a higher charge rate, with Phillips and Brown (forthcoming) finding that 49 per cent of all suspects were charged compared to 53 per cent in the current study. The main cause of this change is likely to be a 1994 Home Office circular together with ACPO guidance which advised forces against the use of multiple cautions. In this context adult cautions remained relatively stable (12% compared to 13% in Phillips and Brown's study), however juveniles cautions fell from 34 per cent to 26 per cent in the current research – a decline of just under a quarter. The existence of a new, lower rate of cautioning is supported by other work conducted during the mid-1990s (see Evans and Ellis, 1996). This drop in cautioning has been almost totally transferred to the charge category, with the rate for juveniles increasing from 33 per cent in Phillips and Brown's study to 40 per cent in the current study. Juvenile suspects are therefore more likely to face a formal disposal than in the past.

Key points

- Just over half of all suspects were charged (53%), 15 per cent were cautioned, 19 per cent NFAed, and the remaining 13 per cent transferred or released.

- A number of important changes were found in the way juvenile suspects were treated, these included:

  - a reduction in juveniles being bailed for enquiries or reported for summons

  - a reduction in police forces diverting juveniles away from prosecution

  - a reduction in the juveniles cautioned (from 34 to 26%)

  - a rise in juveniles charged (from 33 to 40%).

  Differences between juvenile and adult suspects were therefore much less distinct than in the past. These developments were mainly due to a 1994 Home Office circular concerning cautioning policy.

- Comparison with previous research indicates that the level of charging for serious or moderate offences remains broadly the same. However, the figure for minor offences appears to have declined noticeably, with a corresponding rise in cases being NFAed.

- Wide variations were found in the pattern of disposals between stations, with charge rates ranging from 34 per cent at Croydon to 68 per cent at Radford Road. However, comparison with previous studies suggest that these variations are much less than in the past: for example, cautioning rates between stations were found to be much more consistent.

7 Bail or custody?

After a suspect is charged, the custody officer must decide whether to grant bail or detain that person them prior to their first court appearance. This decision is based on what the custody officer is told by the arresting or investigating officers and on other information, such as the suspect's previous record of appearing at court and offending on bail. If the custody officer decides that bail should be granted, this may be with or without conditions. Of those suspects in the custody record sample who were charged:

- 63 per cent were unconditionally bailed;

- 17 per cent were conditionally bailed; and

- 20 per cent were detained in police custody.

This chapter pays particular attention to the use of bail with conditions. Once only available to the courts, the police were given an equivalent power in the CJPOA.

Detention after charge

In the past bail could be refused for a number of specific reasons. One of these involved the belief that the accused may cause physical harm, loss or damage if released. While this covered a large number of offences it did not extend to certain types, including drug and drink-driving offences. This meant that those charged with such offences would be automatically released despite the likelihood that they would be placed in detention having appeared at court. Section 28 of the CJPOA sought to address this anomaly by amending s38(1) of PACE and adding an additional reason for refusing bail. Bail can now be refused to a person charged with an imprisonable offence, where the custody officer has reasonable grounds for believing that this is necessary to prevent that person committing a further offence. At the same time detention based on the possibility of physical harm, loss or damage is now restricted to non-imprisonable offences.

Reasons for refusing bail are outlined according to type of offence in Table

7.1. This table shows that the possibility of further offences being committed is used as grounds for detention in around a third of all cases in which bail is refused. This and the suspicion that the accused will fail to appear at court were the most common reasons for detention after charge. Those accused of offences against the person were most likely to be detained in order to prevent further offences and to prevent any interference in the case, with fears concerning witness intimidation most likely to surround these suspects. Those accused of property offences were most likely to be detained in order to prevent further offences and to prevent any failure to appear at court. Research carried out before the new bail provisions found that the risk of a suspect committing injury, loss or damage were formerly the most common reasons for detention after charge (see Phillips and Brown, forthcoming). This ground is now relatively little used.

Table 7.1 Reasons for refusing bail

Reason	Offences against the person	Property offences	All offences
	%	%	%
Prevent further offences (imprisonable offences)	29	35	32
Risk of failure to appear at court	19	34	31
Risk of interference with the administration of justice/ investigation of the offence	28	6	13
Risk of physical harm, loss or damage (non-imprisonable offences)	12	11	11
Name or address could not be ascertained	6	9	9
For accused's own protection	6	1	2
Detention of juvenile in own interests	•	4	2

Notes:
1. Sample size= 988 (suspects detained after charge).
2. Figures add up to more than 100 per cent due to multiple reasons given.
3. Offences against the person=violence against the person, sexual offences and robbery. Property offences=burglary, theft and handling, and criminal damage.
4. • =less than one per cent.

As highlighted in previous studies, the proportion of those detained after charge varies from station to station (see Brown, 1989; Phillips and Brown, forthcoming). Variations in the custody record sample ranged from eight per cent at Beaumont Leys and Wolverhampton to 31 per cent at Rochdale. Such variations are partly accounted for by the types of offences found at each station. As expected, serious offences were most likely to involve detention, with bail being refused in a third of cases. Of these, robbery and sexual offences were most likely to involve detention after charge (41 and 39%, respectively); violent offences were much less likely to involve detention (17%). Other offences with high detention rates included aggravated 'TWOC' (taking a vehicle without the owner's consent) (34%) and household burglary (31%).

Past studies have suggested another factor in variations between stations is the proportion of juveniles among those charged, since these are more likely to be given bail than adults. Phillips and Brown (forthcoming) found that while 23 per cent of adults charged were refused bail, only 12 per cent of juveniles were refused bail. The current study found a very different picture with both groups being detained at the same level (16%), indicating both a drop in adults being refused bail, and a rise for juveniles. The drop for adults may be due to the better targeting of bail, with the growth of bail information schemes. The rise for juveniles may be due to increasing concerns surrounding juveniles offending while on police bail.

Differences were also found in terms of ethnicity: 21 per cent of Afro-Caribbeans were detained after charge, compared to 16 per cent of both whites and Asians. One reason for this relates to the above average number of drugs, robbery and burglary charges among Afro-Caribbean suspects. Such an offence profile also explains differences in the reasons given for detention after charge, with 38 per cent of Afro-Caribbeans detained because of concerns about interference with the administration of justice, compared to 17 per cent of whites. Only nine per cent of women were detained after charge compared to 19 per cent of men. Again the types of offences involved mainly explain this difference, with women more likely to be charged with offences which were unlikely to justify further detention such as theft, fraud and forgery, and prostitution. Of those women refused bail, 25 per cent were detained because their name and address could not be ascertained, compared to 14 per cent of men.

Bail with conditions

When a custody officer is unwilling to grant bail, an accused person will be detained in custody and brought before court where they can make a bail application. The court might then grant bail, often with conditions. In an attempt to save court time and cut down on overnight remand prisoners, the RCCJ recommended that the power to place conditions on bail should be extended to the police. The CJPOA amended s47 of PACE accordingly. This section examines firstly the extent to which police officers now use bail with conditions, and whether as a consequence of the new legislation fewer people spend time in detention once charged. Secondly, the kinds of conditions placed on those bailed are explored.

Use of bail with conditions

Of those charged, 17 per cent were given bail with conditions. However, the use of bail with conditions has not substantially reduced the proportion of suspects detained after charge. Phillips and Brown (forthcoming), in a study immediately preceding the new legislation, found that 22 per cent of those charged were detained for court. The present study found only a very small decline in this proportion, with 20 per cent of suspects now being detained after charge. The fact that bail with conditions is being used so frequently implies that it is now being used for people who in the past would have been charged and released unconditionally. This finding confirms other research on police bail with conditions, which suggests that police officers appear cautious about taking on the extra responsibility of granting bail in cases where there is a possibility of breach or reoffending (see Raine and Willson, 1996). In such cases officers still decide on detention overnight, deferring responsibility for bail to magistrates the next day.

Figure 7.1 provides figures relating to bail and detention according to the seriousness of the offence. Bail with conditions was most likely to be granted in serious cases; just over four out of ten suspects charged with serious offences were released on this basis, compared to two out of ten charged with moderately serious offences and one out of ten charged with minor offences. Bail with conditions was most likely to be used in cases of threats/conspiracy to murder, GBH, ABH, common assault and indecent assault, and least likely to be used in drug and motoring cases (6 and 5%, respectively).

Figure 7.1 Bail and detention for suspects charged according to type of offence

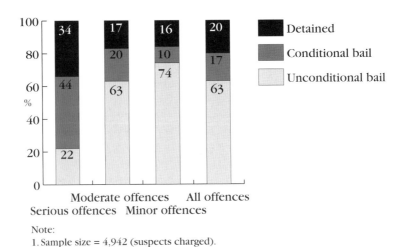

Note:
1. Sample size = 4,942 (suspects charged).

There were significant differences in the use of bail between stations, with for example 30 per cent of those charged at Luton conditionally bailed compared to two per cent at Romford.[1] Such differences could also occur within the same force, with 23 per cent of suspects charged at Brierley Hill conditionally bailed compared to eight per cent at Wolverhampton. The kinds offences found at each station played a large part in such variations, however it was clear that the same offence might be treated differently across stations. For example, at Luton a large proportion of those charged with ABH, TWOC and criminal damage were released on conditional bail, while at Beaumont Leys such suspects tended to be unconditionally released. This may be partly due to those factors, other than seriousness of the offence, considered by custody officers when making a decision about bail. These may include previous criminal record, recent patterns of offending, previous appearance record, previous offending on bail, information from the officer in the case, and legal adviser's representations. However, police practice was likely to be an important factor, with a greater willingness among some station's custody officers to use this type of bail, together with informal policies on the kinds of offence bail where conditions should be used.

Women were less likely to be given conditional bail compared to men (11 and 17% respectively); however this was because they were more likely to be charged and unconditionally released. Conditional bail was given to 22 per cent of Asians, compared to 15 per cent of both whites and Afro-Caribbeans; this appeared to be linked to an above average number of public order offences among Asians, with attached conditions for this group more likely to include keeping away from a victim's address compared to whites and Afro-Caribbeans. Interestingly the age of suspects at each station did not appear to be a strong factor in explaining variations in the use of conditional bail. It might be expected that concerns about juveniles offending while on bail would lead to bail with attached conditions being used disproportionately among this group. Surprisingly, however, juveniles were only slightly more likely to be given bail with conditions (17%), than adults (15%).

Conditions attached to bail

Table 7.2 shows the kind of conditions that officers attached to bail according to the offence, on average two requirements with attached in each case. Overall, six out of ten of those released on bail with conditions were told not to contact named individuals, including witnesses and victims. Six out of ten were also told to keep away from named places, such as a local town centre, a victim's address and licensed premises. Smaller proportions

---

1   Raine and Willson's study confirms Luton's greater use of conditional bail compared to the other stations.

were told to keep a curfew between specific hours, report to the local police station, or reside at a specific address.

Table 7.2 Conditions attached to police bail by offence

Conditions	Offences against person	Property offences	Public order offences	All offences
	%	%	%	%
Not to contact victims/ witnesses	100	41	63	67
Keep away from named places	74	53	89	61
Curfew between specific hours	22	46	2	33
Report to local police station	3	33	0	16
Reside at a specific address	4	12	14	7
Other	3	12	2	11

Notes:
1. Sample size= 840 (suspects conditionally bailed after charge).
2. Offences against the person=violence against the person, sexual offences and robbery. Property offences=burglary, theft and handling, and criminal damage. Public order offences=violent disorder, affray, breach of the peace and drunk and disorderly.
3. Figures add up to more than 100 per cent due to multiple conditions attached to bail.

All of those charged with offences against the person were told not to contact named individuals. This condition concerned victims in 56 per cent of cases and witnesses in 44 per cent. Seven out of ten of these suspects were also told to keep away from named places, this normally being the victim's address. Over a half of suspects charged with property offences were told to keep away from named places, these tending to be town centres in cases of shoplifting and a victim's address in cases of burglary. Nearly nine out of ten suspects charged with public order offences were told to keep away from named places – usually a particular house, pub, night-club, football ground or victim's address.

Reasons for conditional bail

Table 7.3 presents the reasons for attaching conditions to bail. In over six out of ten cases conditions were placed on bail because custody officers believed the accused might offend again. In over half of all cases, conditions were placed on bail because officers believed the accused might interfere in the case by contacting witnesses or the victim. The possibility of the person charged failing to appear at the end of the bail period was much less of a concern among officers. This is important, bearing in mind that bail with conditions is viewed as a replacement for custody in some cases.

Table 7.3 Reasons for conditional bail

Reasons	Offences against person	Property offences	Public order offences	All offences
	%	%	%	%
Prevent offending on bail	62	77	55	67
Prevent interference with justice	77	35	71	54
Prevent failure to appear	5	14	7	13

Notes:
1. Sample size=840 (suspects conditionally bailed after charge).
2. Offences against the person include violence against the person, sexual offences and robbery. Property offences include burglary, theft and handling, and criminal damage. Public order offences include violent disorder, breach of the peace and drunk and disorderly.
3. Figures add up to more than 100 per cent due to multiple reasons given for conditional bail.

Reasons for conditional bail varied according to the type of offence. For example, the belief that the suspect might interfere with justice was cited in seven out of ten cases involving offences against the person and public order offences, highlighting concerns in these cases about victims and witnesses being intimidated. However, interference with justice was only cited in a third of cases involving property offences. Despite such variations, the concern that the accused might offend while on bail was cited in the majority of all cases, but especially for those involving property offences.

Key points

- Of those suspects charged, 63 per cent were bailed conditionally, 17 per cent were bailed with conditions, and 20 per cent were detained in custody. The refusal of bail and the granting of bail with conditions occurred at broadly the same rate for juveniles and adults.

- The most common reason for suspects being detained after charge was to prevent further offences. However, the risks that the suspect may fail to appear or may interfere with police investigations were also cited as important grounds for refusing bail.

- The proportion of suspects detained after charge varied between stations and according to offence, with the highest refusal rate being found in robbery and sexual offences.

- The introduction of police bail with conditions has had only a limited impact on detention after charge. Instead conditions appeared to be placed on those people who would in the past have been bailed unconditionally.

- Bail with conditions was most likely to be given in serious offences against the person. There were significant variations in its use between stations.

- The most common conditions attached to bail were not to contact victims or witnesses, and to keep away from certain, named places. The main reasons given for these conditions were to prevent offending on bail and to prevent interference with justice.

8 Conclusion

The main aim of this study was to examine changes in the revised PACE Codes of Practice concerning those in police detention. It also sought to investigate other related changes arising from the CJPOA and to monitor a number of aspects in the operation of PACE. In this concluding chapter the main findings of the research are discussed along with their implications.

Appropriate adults

In line with the Codes of Practice appropriate adults were provided in the majority of cases involving juvenile and mentally disordered or handicapped detainees[1]. However, shortcomings were found in the level of guidance provided to appropriate adults. Custody officers rarely gave advice to those acting as appropriate adults about the role, and were unlikely to be asked for any. The implication of this lack of guidance is that a large proportion of those acting as appropriate adults, particular those other than social workers, probably do not know what their role actually is, and could be said to be acting as appropriate adults in name only.

The research also examined the suitability of those acting as appropriate adults for juvenile detainees. Here the reactions of family members on finding a child in police custody could undermine their ability to be an appropriate adult. Notable proportions of family members were found to be distressed or hostile to the juvenile, leading to various reactions including remoteness, antagonism and, in some cases, violence. In slightly more cases family members were described as either supportive or calm. However, such demeanours did not mean that the appropriate adult role was adequately fulfilled. As revealed by other research (see Palmer and Hart, 1996; Evans, 1993) many parents were simply passive observers, making few or no interventions and providing little advice or assistance to the juvenile. The actions of those who became involved revealed their confusion about the role, with some parents advising their children to remain silent and others encouraging them to confess. The effectiveness of parents acting as appropriate adults and providing a safeguard is an important issue. Juveniles represent around *one in five detainees* and parents act as appropriate adults in the majority of cases. The research also raised questions about the suitability of those other than family members acting as appropriate adults.

---

1   Although the level of provision was much lower for mentally disordered detainees compared to juveniles.

Concerns about the role of appropriate adults led the RCCJ to recommend a comprehensive review of the role, functions, qualifications, training and availability of appropriate adults. This review was instituted by the Home Office in 1994. The resulting Appropriate Adults Working Group was also asked to consider three other issues. Firstly, the changes to Code C needed to give effect to any recommendations. Secondly, whether the police required clearer guidance about the criteria to be used in considering the need for an appropriate adult. Thirdly, and following another RCCJ recommendation, whether there was a need for a rule governing the status of information passed by suspects to appropriate adults. The Working Group reported in mid-1995 and made a series of wide ranging recommendations which are currently under consideration. A future Home Office circular will provide the police with further guidance on appropriate adults, with associated changes possibly being made to the Codes of Practice.

Legal advice

Studies since the introduction of PACE have indicated rises in suspects requesting legal advice. The current study found a further increase, with four out of ten suspects now making requests. One explanation for this is the increase in requests among juvenile suspects. However, the level of legal advice actually received was only slightly higher than in previous studies, indicating a rise in the attrition rate. Reasons given by suspects for refusing legal advice were rarely recorded by custody officers; in those cases where they were, the majority of suspects simply said that the situation did not merit it.

Comparisons with previous research suggest that legal consultations have increased in duration. The changes to the right of silence mean that suspects in custody require sound legal advice on their position when being questioned by officers. As a result legal advisers need to take time to guide their clients on how to respond to police questions in the context of the inferences that may be drawn from silence. The quality of legal advice received by suspects has been the source of some criticism in the past, notably surrounding the use of unqualified legal staff. As a result the Law Society introduced a scheme whereby those passing a series of tests can become 'accredited representatives' and receive the same status as solicitors. The current study indicates that the proportion of unqualified legal staff advising at police stations has declined, due to a rise in solicitors attending and the introduction of 'accredited representatives'. Whether this development has led to any improvement in the legal advice suspects receive remains unclear.

The right of silence

The extent to which suspects used the right of silence was found to have declined compared to estimates from studies conducted before the new provisions. 'No comment' interviews were found to have fallen by just under a half, while the selective answering of questions had fallen by just under a third. Reductions in the use of silence were found to be greatest among those receiving legal advice. However, confessions by suspects during interviews remained at the same level as before the new provisions. Suspects therefore appear to be responding to police questions without making admissions of guilt any more than before. One possibility is that more suspects are providing officers with statements which, while not admissions of guilt, can be tested against other evidence. The full implications of the new provisions will depend on what happens in the prosecution and trial processes; however these will be addressed in a forthcoming report which will provide further information from this research and other work.

Disposal of juvenile suspects

One of the most pronounced developments found in the study concerned juveniles. Probably as a result of a Home Office circular advising against multiple cautions, juveniles were more likely to be charged and less likely to be cautioned. Furthermore decisions on juveniles were made much earlier in the process than in the past. Consequently, there was a decline in juveniles being bailed for inquiries or reported for summons, with disposal decisions being increasingly made at the end of detention. Finally, once charged juveniles were more likely than before to be refused bail and detained for court.

These developments have a number of consequences. First, juveniles are less likely to be diverted away from prosecution than in the past. This is linked to a decline in the role of juvenile bureaux or panels, with decisions on juvenile cases increasingly the sole responsibility of police officers. Second, changes in the disposal of juveniles together with the rise in their requests for legal advice, means that previous divisions in the treatment of juvenile and adult suspects appear much less distinct. Third, these developments mean that a greater number of juveniles will be at liberty having been charged by the police and bailed pending various court appearances. An unintended consequence of this may be a rise in the levels of offending on bail.

DNA sampling

Alterations to the Codes of Practice have provided far greater scope for DNA sampling, with officers now able to take samples from a much larger range of suspects than in the past. However, the study found samples to be taken from a relatively small proportion of suspects. Clearly intimate samples were only taken in very specific cases, while non-intimate samples were also taken selectively. This may be due to ACPO and Home Office guidance advising that non-intimate samples should only be taken for certain types of crime (i.e. offences against the person, sexual offences and burglaries). Samples were taken for other forms of crime, although it is likely that the suspects concerned had previous links to the offences in the designated categories. The vast majority of samples were taken in order to build up the DNA database and, while the proportion of suspects sampled appears relatively small, it should be noted that approximately 1.5 million people enter police custody every year. Selective sampling therefore is likely to add a substantial number of people to the database over the forthcoming years.

Appendix A

Table A.1 Proportion of requests for legal advice by station

Station	Suspects %	Other detainees %	Total %
Basingstoke	43	52	44
Beaumont Leys	46	55	47
Bedford	40	33	39
Brierley Hill	27	21	26
Cambridge	31	33	31
Campbell Square	46	66	49
Charles Street	45	56	46
Corby	41	38	40
Coventry	37	38	37
Croydon	36	35	36
Gateshead	42	57	46
Hackney	43	37	42
Lewisham	39	37	39
Luton	43	38	42
Newcastle East	33	29	32
Newcastle West	40	27	36
Nottingham Central	47	70	52
Peterborough	44	48	44
Queens Road	47	49	48
Radford Road	57	64	57
Rochdale	34	31	33
Romford	31	18	30
Southampton	35	49	37
Stretford	44	42	44
Wolverhampton	19	26	20
Total	40	42	40

Note:
1. Sample size=4,144 (suspects requesting legal advice); 823 (other detainees requesting legal advice); 4,967 (both groups together).

Table A.2 Proportion of suspects requesting legal advice by offence

Offence	%
Violence	52
Sexual	59
Burglary	57
Robbery	65
Theft and handling	40
Shoplifting	29
Theft of vehicles	54
Theft from vehicles	46
TWOCs	52
Other theft and handling	41
Fraud and forgery	49
Criminal damage	39
Drugs	37
Public order	30
Motoring offences	26
Prostitution	5
Miscellaneous	59
Other offences	51
Total	40

Note:
1. Sample size= 4,144 (suspects requesting legal advice).

Table A.3 Length of consultations between legal advisers and suspects

Length of consultation Minutes	%
Less than 5	7
from 5 to less than 10	21
from 10 to less than 15	21
from 15 to less than 30	34
from 30 to less than 45	10
from 45 to less than 60	5
from 60 to less than 90	2

Note:
1. Sample size= 1,201 (suspects receiving consultations at police stations).

Table A.4 Frequency of police interviews with suspects

No. of interviews	Offence for which suspect arrested			
	Serious	Moderate	Minor	All
	%	%	%	%
1	81	88	95	90
2	14	11	5	9
3	3	2	1	1
4 or more	2	•	0	•
Total	100	100	100	100

Note:
1. Sample size=7,820 (serious offences: 360; moderate offences: 5,974; minor offences: 1,546).
2. •= less than one per cent.

Table A.5 Extent of legal advice for suspects interviewed by police officers according to station

Station	Legal adviser at all interviews	Legal adviser at some interviews	Advice given pre-interview only	No legal advice given
	%	%	%	%
Beaumont Leys	44	5	4	47
Campbell Sq	8	1	30	61
Croydon	43	2	8	47
Gateshead	29	2	4	65
Hackney	53	0	6	41
Luton	31	2	17	50
Peterborough	53	2	2	43
Queens Road	40	2	5	53
Radford Road	47	1	2	50
Rochdale	39	2	1	58
Southampton	29	2	16	53
Stretford	51	2	3	44
Wolverhampton	34	2	3	61
Total	37	2	9	52

Note:
1. Sample size= 2,181 (suspects interviewed).

Table A.6 Outcome of detention for adults by station

Station	Charge	Instant caution	Summons	Bail	NFA	Other
	%	%	%	%	%	%
Bedford	53	11	•	12	19	5
Luton	51	7	0	9	24	9
Cambridge	39	13	1	19	24	4
Peterborough	50	11	1	10	25	3
Rochdale	62	10	3	7	10	8
Stretford	62	10	•	4	16	8
Basingstoke	54	9	12	2	18	5
Southampton	48	13	10	6	18	5
Charles St	53	14	1	13	15	4
Beaumont Leys	55	5	2	13	19	6
Croydon	34	16	1	17	28	4
Hackney	41	16	3	8	30	2
Lewisham	36	15	1	16	26	6
Romford	43	13	•	17	22	5
Corby	52	13	3	5	21	6
Campbell Sq	61	9	5	6	13	6
Gateshead	54	10	2	6	17	11
Newcastle East	51	17	3	6	17	6
Newcastle West	53	12	3	7	18	7
Radford Road	68	6	1	8	12	5
Notts Central	66	6	1	7	15	5
Brierley Hill	52	13	•	7	21	7
Coventry	57	13	•	14	10	6
Queens Road	54	9	1	21	10	5
Wolverhampton	60	14	•	6	14	6
Total	52	11	2	10	19	6

Notes:
1. Sample size= 8,160 (adult suspects).
2. •= less than one per cent.

Table A.7 Outcome of detention for adults by police force

Force	Charge	Instant caution	Summons	Bail	NFA	Other
	%	%	%	%	%	%
Bedfordshire	52	9	•	11	21	7
Cambridgeshire	45	12	1	15	24	3
GMP	61	10	2	6	13	8
Hampshire	51	11	11	4	18	5
Leicestershire	54	10	1	13	17	5
Metropolitan	39	15	1	14	27	4
Northamptonshire	56	11	4	6	17	6
Northumbria	53	13	3	6	17	8
Nottinghamshire	68	6	1	7	13	5
West Midlands	56	12	•	12	14	6
Total	52	11	2	10	19	6

Notes:
1. Sample size= adult suspects (8,160).
2. Table excludes juvenile suspects.

Table A.8 Outcome of detention for juveniles by police force

Force	Charge	Instant caution	Summons	Bail	NFA	Other
	%	%	%	%	%	%
Bedfordshire	31	31	1	11	25	1
Cambridgeshire	30	16	0	26	27	1
GMP	48	18	•	10	19	5
Hampshire	16	25	40	1	17	1
Leicestershire	26	28	4	14	26	2
Metropolitan	23	25	1	26	23	2
Northamptonshire	19	4	19	8	43	7
Northumbria	42	16	5	11	22	4
Nottinghamshire	53	15	0	13	17	2
West Midlands	30	17	•	25	26	2
Total	33	19	5	16	24	3

Notes:
1. Sample size= juvenile suspects (2,135).
2. • =less than one percent.
3. Table excludes adults suspects.

Appendix B

Model of seriousness of the offence

The classification of offences used in the model by Brown et al. (1992) was expanded upon.

Very serious offences:

Murder
Attempted Murder
Threat or conspiracy to murder
Manslaughter
Causing death by dangerous driving
Grevious bodily harm
Rape
Indecent assault on female
Gross indecency
Attempted abduction
Kidnapping
Blackmail
Riot

Moderately serious offences:

Actual Bodily Harm
Other violence
Indecent assault on male
Indecency between males
Other sexual offences
Burglary dwelling
Burglary other
Aggravated burglary
Robbery assault with intent to rob
Taking without the owner's consent
Aggravated vehicle taking
Theft from motor vehicle

Theft from person
Theft of pedal cycle
Theft of motor vehicle
Theft other
Theft from employer
Abstracting electricity
Going equipped
Found in enclosed premises
Interference with motor vehicle
Handling stolen goods
Fraud false accounting
Forgery
Obtaining goods / services by deception
Arson
Criminal damage – over £20
Criminal damage – value not known
Production / supply of controlled drug
Possession of controlled drug
Violent disorder
Affray
Fear / provocation of violence
Other public order
Dangerous driving
Careless driving resulting in death
Careless driving
Driving after consuming drugs or alcohol
Driving whilst disqualified
Absconding from lawful custody
Perverting the course of justice

Less serious offences:

Common assault
Assault on constable
Prostitution
Shoplifting
Criminal damage – £20 or less
Harassment / alarm / distress
Breach of the peace
Drunk and disorderly
Drunk and incapable
Vagrancy
Obstruction of police

Indecent exposure
Possession of offensive weapon
Other licence insurance / documentation
Speeding
Other motoring
Failure to appear at court
Immigration offences
Miscellaneous offences
Warrant – non payment of fine
Warrant – failure to appear
Breach of injunction
S.48 PACE remand
Refusal to provide a specimen
S.25 PACE

References

Association of Chief Police Officers. (1993) *ACPO Right of Silence Survey* (unpublished).

Association of Chief Police Officers. (1995). *Memorandum of Understanding. National DNA Database*. Unpublished.

Brown, D. (1989). *Detention at the Police Station under the Police and Criminal Evidence Act 1984*. Home Office Research Study No. 104, London: HMSO.

Brown, D. (1991). *Investigating Burglary: The Effects of PACE*. Home Office Research Study No.123. London: HMSO.

Brown, D. (1994). *'The incidence of right of silence in police interviews: the research evidence reviewed'*. Research Bulletin, No. 35, 57-75. London: Home Office Research and Statistics Department.

Brown, D. (1997). *PACE Ten Years on: A Review of the Research*. Home Office Research Study No. 155. London: HMSO.

Brown, D., Ellis, T. and Larcombe, K. (1992). *Changing the Code: Police Detention under the Revised PACE Codes of Practice*. Home Office Research Study No. 129. London: HMSO.

Bottomley, K., Coleman, C., Dixon, D., Gill, M. and Wall, D. (1989). *The Impact of Aspects of the Police and Criminal Evidence Act 1984 on Policing in a Force in the North of England*. Final report to ESRC. Unpublished.

Card, R. and Ward, R. (1994). *The Criminal Justice and Public Order Act 1994*. Bristol: Jordans.

Dixon, D., Bottomley, K., Coleman, C., Gill, M. and Wall, D. (1990). *'Safeguarding the rights of suspects in police custody'*. Policing and Society, (1), 115-40.

Evans, R. (1993). *The Conduct of Police Interviews with Juveniles.* Royal Commission on Criminal Justice Research Study No. 8. London: HMSO.

Evans, R. and Ellis, R (1996). *Police Cautioning in England and Wales.* A report to the Home Office Research and Statistics Directorate. Unpublished.

Evans, R. and Rawstorne, S. (1994). *The Protection of Vulnerable Suspects.* A report to the Home Office Research and Planning Unit. Unpublished.

Gudjunsson, G., Clare, I., Rutter, S. and Pearse, J. (1993). *Persons at Risk during Interviews in Police Custody: the identification of vulnerabilities.* Royal Commission on Criminal Justice Research Study No 12. London: HMSO.

Home Office (1995). *National DNA Database. Circular 16/95.* London: HMSO.

Home Office (1996). *Criminal Statistics 1995.* Cm 3421. London: HMSO.

Irving, B.L. and McKenzie, I. (1989). *Police Interrogation: the effects of the Police and Criminal Evidence Act 1984.* London: Police Foundation.

Leng, R. (1994). *'The Right-to-Silence Debate'.* In Morgan, D. and Stephenson, G.S. *Suspicion and Silence.* London: Blackwell.

McConville, M. (1993). *Corroboration and Confessions: the impact of a rule requiring that no conviction can be sustained on the basis of confession evidence alone.* Royal Commission on Criminal Justice Research Study No. 13, London: HMSO.

McConville, M. and Hodgson, J, with the assistance of Jackson, M. and Macrae, E. (1993). *Custodial Legal Advice and the Right to Silence.* Royal Commission on Criminal Justice Research Study No. 16. London: HMSO.

McConville, M., Hodgson, J., Bridges, L. and Pavlovic, A. (1994). *Standing Accused: the organisation and practices of criminal defence lawyers in Britain.* Oxford: Clarendon Press.

Morgan, J, Harris, D. and Burrows, J. (1996). *Preliminary Study of the Use of DNA Evidence.* A report to the Home Office Research and Statistics Directorate. Unpublished.

Leng, R. (1993) *The Right of Silence in Police Interrogation: a study of some of the underlying the debate.* Royal Commission on Criminal Justice Research Study No. 10. London: HMSO.

Morgan, R., Reiner, R. and McKenzie, I.K. (1991). *Police Powers and Police: a study of the work of custody officers.* Full final report to the ESRC. Unpublished.

Moston, S. and Stephson, G. (1993). *The Questioning and Interviewing of Suspects outside the Police Station.* Royal Commission on Criminal Justice Research Study No. 22. London: HMSO.

Moston, S., Stephenson, G. and Williamson, T. (1990). *Police Interrogation Styles and Suspect Behaviour. Final report to the Police Requirements Support Unit:* University of Kent, Institute of Social and Applied Psychology. Unpublished.

Palmer, C. (1996). *'The Appropriate Adult'. Legal Action,* May 1996, p6-7.

Palmer, C and Hart, M (1996). *A PACE in the Right Direction?* Sheffield: University of Sheffield.

Phillips, C. and Brown, D., with the assistance of Goodrich, P. and James, Z. (forthcoming). *Entry into the Criminal Justice System: a survey of police arrests and their outcomes.* Home Office Research and Statistics Study. London: HMSO.

Phillips, C. and Brown, D. (1997). *'Observational studies in police custody areas: some methodological and ethical issues considered'.* Policing and Society, (3), p191-205.

Raine, J.W. and Willson, M.J. (1996). *Police Bail with Conditions.* A report to the Home Office Research and Statistics Directorate. Unpublished.

Reiner, R. (1992). *The Politics of the Police.* London: Harvester Wheatsheaf.

Robertson, G., Pearson, R. and Gibb, R. (1995). *Entry of Mentally Ill People to the Criminal Justice System.* Final Report to Home Office Research and Planning Unit. Unpublished.

Sanders, A., Bridges, L., Mulvaney, A. and Crozier, G. (1989). *Advice and Assistance at Police Stations and the 24 hour Duty Solicitor Scheme.* London: Lord Chancellor's Department.

Steventon, B. (1995). *'Creating a DNA Database.' Journal of Criminal Law*, November, 1995, p411–419.

Softley, P., with the assistance of Brown, D., Forde, B., Mair, G. and Moxon, D. (1980). *Police Interrogation: an observational study in four police stations.* Home Office Research Study No. 61. London: HMSO.

Tain, P. (1994). *Criminal Justice and Public Order Act 1994:* A Practical Guide. London: Longman.

Thomas, T. (1988). *'The Police and Criminal Evidence Act 1984: the social work role'.* The Howard Journal of Criminal Justice, Vol. 27, No. 4, pp. 256–265.

Publications

List of research publications

A list of research reports for the last three years is provided below. **A full** list of publications is available on request from the Research and Statistics Directorate Information and Publications Group.

Home Office Research Studies (HORS)

151. **Drug misuse declared: results of the 1994 British Crime Survey.** Malcom Ramsay and Andrew Percy. 1996.

152. **An Evaluation of the Introduction and Operation of the Youth Court.** David O'Mahony and Kevin Haines. 1996.

153. **Fitting supervision to offenders: assessment and allocation decisions in the Probation Service.** 1996.

155. **PACE: a review of the literature. The first ten years.** David Brown. 1997.

156. **Automatic Conditional Release: the first two years.** Mike Maguire, Brigitte Perroud and Peter Raynor. 1996.

157. **Testing obscenity: an international comparison of laws and controls relating to obscene material.** Sharon Grace. 1996.

158. **Enforcing community sentences: supervisors' perspectives on ensuring compliance and dealing with breach.** Tom Ellis, Carol Hedderman and Ed Mortimer. 1996.

160. **Implementing crime prevention schemes in a multi-agency setting: aspects of process in the Safer Cities programme.** Mike Sutton. 1996.

161. **Reducing criminality among young people: a sample of relevant programmes in the United Kingdom.** David Utting. 1997.

162 **Imprisoned women and mothers.** Dianne Caddle and Debbie Crisp. 1996.

163. **Curfew orders with electronic monitoring: an evaluation of the first twelve months of the trials in Greater Manchester, Norfolk and Berkshire, 1995 - 1996.** George Mair and Ed Mortimer. 1996..

164. **Safer cities and domestic burglaries.** Paul Ekblom, Ho Law, Mike Sutton, with assistance from Paul Crisp and Richard Wiggins. 1996.

165. **Enforcing financial penalties.** Claire Whittaker and Alan Mackie. 1997.

166. **Assessing offenders' needs: assessment scales for the probation service.** Rosumund Aubrey and Michael Hough. 1997.

167. **Offenders on probation.** George Mair and Chris May. 1997.

168. **Managing courts effectively: The reasons for adjournments in magistrates' courts.** Claire Whittaker, Alan Mackie, Ruth Lewis and Nicola Ponikiewski. 1997.

169. **Addressing the literacy needs of offenders under probation supervision.** Gwynn Davis et al. 1997.

170. **Understanding the sentencing of women.** edited by Carol Hedderman and Lorraine Gelsthorpe. 1997.

171. **Changing offenders' attitudes and behaviour: what works?** Julie Vennard, Darren Sugg and Carol Hedderman 1997.

172 **Drug misuse declared in 1996: latest results from the British Crime Survey.** Malcolm Ramsay and Josephine Spiller. 1997.

No. 159 is not published yet.

Research Findings

30. **To scare straight or educate? The British experience of day visits to prison for young people.** Charles Lloyd. 1996.

31. **The ADT drug treatment programme at HMP Downview – a preliminary evaluation.** Elaine Player and Carol Martin. 1996.

32. **Wolds remand prison – an evaluation.** Keith Bottomley, Adrian James, Emma Clare and Alison Liebling. 1996.

33. **Drug misuse declared: results of the 1994 British Crime Survey.** Malcolm Ramsay and Andrew Percy. 1996.

34. **Crack cocaine and drugs-crime careers.** Howard Parker and Tim Bottomley. 1996.

35. **Imprisonment for fine default.** David Moxon and Claire Whittaker. 1996.

36. **Fine impositions and enforcement following the Criminal Justice Act 1993.** Elizabeth Charman, Bryan Gibson, Terry Honess and Rod Morgan. 1996.

37. **Victimisation in prisons.** Ian O'Donnell and Kimmett Edgar. 1996.

38 **Mothers in prison.** Dianne Caddle and Debbie Crisp. 1997.

39. **Ethnic minorities, victimisation and racial harassment.** Marian Fitzgerald and Chris Hale. 1996.

40. **Evaluating joint performance management between the police and the Crown Prosecution Service.** Andrew Hooke, Jim Knox and David Portas. 1996.

41. **Public attitudes to drug-related crime**. Sharon Grace. 1996.

42. **Domestic burglary schemes in the safer cities programme**. Paul Ekblom, Ho Law and Mike Sutton. 1996.

43. **Pakistani women's experience of domestic violence in Great Britain.** Salma Choudry. 1996.

44. **Witnesses with learning disabilities**. Andrew Sanders, Jane Creaton, Sophia Bird and Leanne Weber. 1997.

45. **Does treating sex offenders reduce reoffending?** Carol Hedderman and Darren Sugg. 1996.

46. **Re-education programmes for violent men - an evaluation.** Russell Dobash, Rebecca Emerson Dobash, Kate Cavanagh and Ruth Lewis. 1996.

47. **Sentencing without a pre-sentence report**. Nigel Charles, Claire Whittaker and Caroline Ball. 1997.

48 **Magistrates' views of the probation service.** Chris May. 1997.

49. **PACE ten years on: a review of the research**. David Brown. 1997.

50   **Persistent drug–misusing offenders.** Malcolm Ramsay. 1997.

51   **Curfew orders with electronic monitoring: The first twelve months.** Ed Mortimer and George Mair. 1997.

52   **Police cautioning in the 1990s.** Roger Evans and Rachel Ellis. 1997.

53.   **A reconviction study of HMP Grendon Therapeutic Community.** Peter Marshall. 1997.

54.   **Control in category c prisons.** Simon Marshall. 1997.

55.   **The prevalence of convictions for sexual offending.** Peter Marshall. 1997.

56   **Drug misuse declared in 1996: key results from the British Crime Survey.** Malcolm Ramsay and Josephine Spiller. 1997.

57   **The 1996 International Crime Victimisation Survey.** Pat Mayhew and Phillip White. 1997.

58   **The sentencing of women: a section 95 publication.** Carol Hedderman and Lizanne Dowds. 1997.

Occasional Papers

Mental disorder in remand prisoners. Anthony Maden, Caecilia J. A. Taylor, Deborah Brooke and John Gunn. 1996.

An evaluation of prison work and training. Frances Simon and Claire Corbett. 1996.

The impact of the national lottery on the horse-race betting levy. Simon Field. 1996.

Evaluation of a Home Office initiative to help offenders into employment. Ken Roberts, Alana Barton, Julian Buchanan, and Barry Goldson. 1997.

The impact of the national lottery on the horse-race betting levy. Simon Field and James Dunmore. 1997.

Requests for Publications

Home Office Research Studies from 143 onwards, *Research and Planning Unit Papers, Research Findings and Research Bulletins* can be requested, **subject to availability**, from:

Research and Statistics Directorate
Information and Publications Group
Room 201, Home Office
50 Queen Anne's Gate
London SW1H 9AT
Telephone: 0171-273 2084
Fascimile: 0171-222 0211
Internet: http://www.open.gov.uk/home_off/rsd/rsdhome.htm
E-mail: rsd.ha apollo @ gtnet.gov.u.

Occasional Papers can be purchased from:
Home Office
Publications Unit
50 Queen Anne's Gate
London SW1H 9AT
Telephone: 0171 273 2302

Home Office Research Studies prior to 143 can be purchased from:

HMSO Publications Centre

(Mail, fax and telephone orders only)
PO Box 276, London SW8 5DT
Telephone orders: 0171-873 9090
General enquiries: 0171-873 0011
(queuing system in operation for both numbers)
Fax orders: 0171-873 8200

*And also from **HMSO Bookshops***